THE BOY SCOUTS
IN THE GREAT WAR

For my Parents

THE BOY SCOUTS IN THE GREAT WAR

CRAIG ARMSTRONG

Pen & Sword
MILITARY

AN IMPRINT OF PEN & SWORD BOOKS LTD.
YORKSHIRE - PHILADELPHIA

First published in Great Britain in 2021 by
Pen & Sword Military
an imprint of
Pen & Sword Books Ltd
Yorkshire – Philadelphia

ISBN 978 1 52672 324 6

A CIP catalogue record for this book is
available from the British Library.

Typeset by SJmagic DESIGN SERVICES, India.
Printed and bound in the UK by CPI Group (UK) Ltd, Croydon, CR0 4YY.

Pen & Sword Books Limited incorporates the imprints of Atlas, Archaeology,
Aviation, Discovery, Family History, Fiction, History, Maritime, Military, Military
Classics, Politics, Select, Transport, True Crime, Air World, Frontline Publishing,
Leo Cooper, Remember When, Seaforth Publishing, The Praetorian Press,
Wharncliffe Local History, Wharncliffe Transport, Wharncliffe True Crime and
White Owl.

For a complete list of Pen & Sword titles please contact
PEN & SWORD BOOKS LIMITED
47 Church Street, Barnsley, South Yorkshire, S70 2AS, England
E-mail: enquiries@pen-and-sword.co.uk
Website: www.pen-and-sword.co.uk

Or
PEN AND SWORD BOOKS
1950 Lawrence Rd, Havertown, PA 19083, USA
E-mail: Uspen-and-sword@casematepublishers.com
Website: www.penandswordbooks.com

Contents

CHAPTER 1

1914

The Home Front

The outbreak of war was met, by many people, with excitement and enthusiasm and in the early days and weeks there was a substantial rush to the colours. Across Britain, large queues of men formed outside recruitment offices as men tried to enlist. The reasons for enlisting were extremely varied. Loyalty, patriotism, a desire to escape the drudgery of life at home or at work, to escape poverty, a wish to get involved before the war ended, a view that war was the ultimate test of manhood, peer pressure, friendship, all of these and more played a role in recruitment. For older boy scouts an undoubted reason was the fact that they had been inculcated with the belief that honour, loyalty and duty to King and country was of paramount importance.

Many of those involved with the Boy Scouts Association were automatically called up anyway. Large numbers were already members of either the reserves or members of the Territorials. This denuded the association of leadership at a crucial time, but the scouts had been organised to be extremely flexible and adaptable and the associations across the country seemed to adapt with remarkable speed and skill to the situation.

Within days of the war being declared, Boy Scouts across Britain were eagerly mobilising and within three days some 50,000 Boy Scouts were said to be ready to assist the military and civilian authorities in any way required. It was not only the leaders of the organisation who were eager to throw the scouts into the fray but there was great eagerness evinced by the boys themselves with thousands of telegrams being sent to the authorities from Boy Scouts begging to be made use of.

Typical of some of the letters from younger scouts was the extract from one which was published in the *Hampshire Independent* on 15 August 1914. The letter to the War Office read:

> I understand there is a war between England and Germany. I am a Boy Scout, aged 10, and shall be pleased to offer my services. So please send a rifle and ammunition, and when the war is over I will return the rifle and what ammunition I have left.[1]

Quite what use would be made of the Boy Scouts during the war was a subject for some debate in the early days. There were undoubtedly some within the movement who hoped that the boys would be mobilised as a quasi-military force to aid in the protection of Britain, but there were distinct concerns over placing young boys, children, into situations where they might come into contact with danger and even with the enemy. Others wished to utilise the movement to provide a form of civilian labour which could be used to aid the many professional and voluntary groups which were mobilising to provide vital wartime necessities such as healthcare, fundraising or farm work. In the first days of the war Sir Robert Baden-Powell was called into meetings at the War Office to discuss the contribution that the Boy Scouts Association might offer to the war effort. Sir Robert quickly offered 1,000 scouts in each county to assist the Chief Constables in a variety of ways. These duties were to include: aiding communications through despatch riders and signallers; guarding various sites against spies; collecting information regarding supplies and transport capabilities; aiding relief work; helping the families of men who were employed in defence duties or the sick or wounded; establishing first aid, dressing and nursing stations along with refuges, dispensaries and soup kitchens in their club rooms; acting as guides and orderlies; and forwarding dispatches that had been dropped by aircraft.

At the outset of the war Britain had no preparations in place for the necessary tasks of guarding strategically important locations such

Sir Robert and Lady Baden-Powell leaving the War Office. (The Sketch)

as telephone exchanges, railway tracks, bridges and canals. Another important task was the watching of the British coastline in case of enemy raiders or attempts to land spies. These tasks were of vital importance but maintaining these guards would overstretch the already taxed British Army and the Royal Navy along with the non-military coastguard service. Very quickly the leadership of the Boy Scouts Association realised that their lads were ready-made for many of these tasks and their services were volunteered with remarkable alacrity. An anxious government gratefully accepted the offer within twenty-four hours and the scouts and sea scouts immediately began their duty. The scouts who took part in these duties did so with gleeful enthusiasm, seeing themselves as Britain's second line of defence. Indeed, the experience of guard duty further encouraged many of the scouts to enlist as soon as they were able. A large number of the sea scouts who undertook coastal watches, for example, later volunteered for service with the Royal Navy.

In Nottinghamshire, the County Commissioner of Scouts, Sir Lancelot Rolleston, received a communique from Sir Robert Baden-Powell on 7 August asking for the services of 1,000 scouts to aid the authorities. Sir Lancelot was busy with his military duties and passed the request on to the chairman of the Notts. Boy Scouts Association, Mr L.O. Trivett. Mr Trivett received a second communique later that day asking for the services of more scouts to assist in the vital task of helping to gather in the harvest. To relay these messages Mr Trivett toured several towns on 7–8 August and was pleased to find enthusiasm in every location with the local scouts demonstrating a 'keen, loyal spirit, and an impatient desire to be of service to their country in its hour of need'. The leaders of the movement in Nottinghamshire quickly mounted a recruitment campaign encouraging scouts to volunteer their services and in Newark, Mansfield, Retford and Worksop the local troops began a recruitment drive.

The government had quickly recognised the Boy Scouts Association as being a public service non-military body which suitable organisations could apply to make use of. Thus, in the first weeks of the war numerous adverts appeared in the local press across Britain urging such bodies to get in touch with the local organisations. The non-military nature of the government's definition of the Boy Scouts was a fairly nebulous one with the militaristic nature of the movement sometimes being at odds with this definition and with some within the movement being determined to make a military contribution if possible. Indeed, many scouts found themselves aiding the army in defending and patrolling coastal locations in the first days of the war, largely acting as messengers and signallers.

Across Britain local authorities hastily set up War Emergency Committees which were to manage the various aspects of the war in local settings. One of the main problems encountered by these committees was in maintaining communications between the different towns and villages within their district. Once again, it was the boy scout who provided the solution to this serious problem. In peacetime, scout cyclists had been encouraged to thoroughly familiarise themselves with the shortest routes between various places in their districts. Mainly, this was so that scouts could find their way between their own local association headquarters and those of others in their district, but as nearly every town and many villages had their own associations it meant that the scouts built up a wide knowledge base. This knowledge proved to be invaluable and the scout dispatch riders employed by the committees also proved to be invaluable. The training that the scout cyclists had undertaken to earn their cyclist merit badge meant that they had to own a bike in good working condition and be prepared to use it in service to the King, to be able to ride safely, to be able to repair punctures, read road maps and to repeat correctly and accurately a verbal message.

Other vital tasks undertaken by the scouts in the first months of the war included duty at supply depots, acting as orderlies to various civilian authority officers, staffing numerous soldiers' clubs. Boy scouts who had earned the Printer Badge, and therefore had knowledge of the processes and technological aspects of printing, were a godsend to many offices and to national and local authorities.

The Boy Scouts quickly proved their worth in a number of ways. In London, hundreds of scouts began work in the War Office, the India Office, His Majesty's Stationery Office, Scotland Yard, the Central Recruiting Office and the Prince of Wales' Fund at York House. At all of these locations scouts were used as messengers, guided visitors, and carried manuscripts and memoranda. So great was the contribution that the scouts had 150 boys at the War Office alone. They also proved their worth in the mass movement of troops following mobilisation. In this case, scouts acted as guides to troops who were unfamiliar with the area and ran confidential messages on behalf of the military authorities. So useful were these services that one General in command of a division recommended a scout troop for a special commendation for their actions when his men were at a halt.

The declaration of war found many scout troops either enjoying their summer camp or having just returned from it. The fact that the scouts who were in camps across Britain were equipped with cycles, signalling equipment, camping equipment, etc, meant that they could very quickly respond to immediate calls for aid which came from both the civil and military authorities. Once again, this rapid deployment was aided by the simplicity of the association's organisation. The localised focus of the organisation, with district commissioners and other local officers, enabled the officers at the head of county groups to quickly establish where they could best deploy the manpower available to them.

This simple but versatile organisation continued at the troop level with each troop being under the command of a scoutmaster and divided into two patrols of eight or more scouts. Each patrol was under a patrol leader who was a boy aged between 11-18. Thus, the district commissioners and the scoutmasters were the backbone of the movement. This did present some difficulties as a great many of these appointed officers were either Territorials, members of the Reserve or immediately enlisted at the beginning of the war. Such officers proved hard to replace and this was a constant problem in the early months.

The speed with which the association acted was remarkable. In St Albans, for example, a meeting of the Hertfordshire County Commissioners was held on Saturday 8 August at which it was agreed to place 1,000 scouts at the disposal of the Chief Constable. The following day the officers from St Albans held their own meeting at which they agreed to mobilise all six St Albans Troops and to have them gather at the headquarters as one body on the following morning. They would be used to give assistance to the local authorities, whether day or night. Letters were sent out to all of the local authorities informing them that the scouts had been organised to provide support where needed. To prepare them, the scouts themselves were gathered at the commissioner's house on the Sunday afternoon and informed of the decisions that had been taken. They were asked to volunteer their services and all of the 130 scouts immediately did so. The boys were organised into three day watches of four hours each and one night watch which would be in place from 8 pm to 6 am. Even before the boys had officially gathered there was a request for a scout to take dispatches to Clapham. This came through on the Sunday and the duty was fulfilled. Such actions were undertaken in nearly every city across Britain.

For all the simplicity and commitment of the commissioners and scoutmasters, it is clear that the amazing response of the movement was dependent upon the enthusiasm and commitment of the scouts themselves. Without the loyalty and commitment to duty which had been instilled in these boys it would have been impossible for the association to make the contribution that it did. The example of the St Alban scouts given above where every available scout immediately committed to the effort was repeated in the majority of locations.

Although we have seen how the Boy Scouts Association was anxious to avoid the insinuation that the movement was a militaristic one, there were those who clearly believed that it was just that. Soon after the outbreak of war, Lord Kitchener had a conversation with Sir Robert Baden-Powell in which he praised the movement as a great national asset, but also said that the war had given the opportunity to show the boys in the scouts what their training was for and that in the situation in which the country found itself it was necessary for every available man to do his utmost for his country.

Although the association had many enthusiastic members there was not universal approval, or even acknowledgement, of the value of the movement. In many parts of the country an ambivalent attitude ruled, while in others there was the contemptuous belief that the boy scouts were merely playing at being soldiers or were being trained to be subservient to authority.

During the first weeks of war this contemptuous attitude could lead to problems. In one case a passing cyclist, with the assumption that the boy scouts guarding the telephone network were merely boys at play, decided it would be funny to climb one of the poles; he was horrified when the nearest scout, whose orders to desist he had disobeyed, sprang forward, drew a pocket-knife, and slashed his bicycle tyres to make sure that he could not make a speedy getaway.

There were also some instances where members of the public thought it might be humorous to dress up as a scoutmaster in order to give orders to local scouts, but the government quickly acted to prevent this. By recognising both the Boy Scouts and the Sea Scouts (and their uniforms) as a public service, non-military body, the government made it illegal for anyone from outside these organisations to wear their uniform.

Others were suspicious of the scouts as they thought that it might be designed to inculcate religious beliefs in gullible boys. Once again, the movement denied this, saying that the religion encouraged was not of any sect (in fact all sects were welcomed), but was summed up by the commitment that every scout made upon joining the association. These were: 'to do my duty to God and the King; to help other people at all times; and to obey the Scout Law.' The Scout Law consisted of ten directives:

The Scout Laws.

1. A Scout's honour is to be trusted.
2. A Scout is loyal the King, his country, his officers, his parents, his employers, and to those under him.
3. A Scout's duty is to be useful and to help others.
4. A Scout is a friend to all, and a brother to every other Scout, no matter to what social class the other belongs.
5. A Scout is courteous.
6. A Scout is a friend to animals.
7. A Scout obeys the orders of his parents, patrol leader, or Scoutmaster without question.

8. A Scout smiles and whistles under all difficulties.
9. A Scout is thrifty.
10. A Scout is clean in thought, word, and deed.

One of the many duties undertaken by scouts in the first days and weeks of the war was to provide aid to non-enemy foreigners who had been left stranded in Britain by the declaration of war. In London, scouts were posted at the American Embassy and at the Savoy Hotel and provided aid to many American nationals who came seeking advice about how to return home. It was not only the bewildered American visitors who were assisted, however. The American ambassador, presenting several scouts with medals later, told the press how the scouts had been of great use and reassurance to the embassy staff. The ambassador praised the scouts for their level-headedness, authority and politeness, while assuring watching pressmen that there was nothing at all militaristic about either the movement or the boys.

Across the country scouts volunteered to aid beleaguered farmers in gathering in the harvest. This was an especially vital task given the number of men from agricultural districts who had been mobilised with the Territorials. However, there was some concern in some quarters that farmers would use the boys as a source of free or extremely cheap labour at the expense of agricultural workers. The authorities were at pains to point out that this was not what was intended. Several London troops volunteered their services to farmers within a thirty-mile radius of Westminster. All that was asked for in return was food and drink, a roof over their heads, and 'possibly (not necessarily) a small money payment'. The scouts would, in most cases, cycle to the farm to save on train fairs and passenger capacity. The London secretary pointed out in the adverts that were placed in the press that this service was only for farmers who had been unable to procure labour owing to local men being called up for the war and that the Scouts' 'good turn' was 'never intended to displace any who may be working for their living'.[2]

One of the quasi-military duties which fell to scouts in the early weeks of the war was that of providing guards over non-vital but still locally important sites such as culverts, bridges and railway embankments. Many of these boys were issued with staffs and given rudimentary training and instructions and were instructed to immediately dispatch a messenger if anything untoward occurred. Many of these messengers acted as dispatch-riders being equipped with a bicycle to aid them in their duties.

In Wales, as elsewhere in Britain, troops of Boy Scouts were dispatched to mount day and night guard over lakes and reservoirs. They were there in case enemy spies tried to poison the country's water supply. In Breconshire, Boy Scouts assisted newly sworn-in Special Constables in guarding the Cardiff Waterworks, while in the Barry district a troop was assigned to guard the local reservoir and Boy Scouts patrolling the district became a common sight. The guarding of a variety of waterworks became commonplace across Britain with

Scouts guarding a culvert. (The Sphere)

Guarding the railway embankment above the culvert. (The Sphere)

270 THE SPHERE [SEPTEMBER 12, 1914

A Despatch Rider Handing in his Message

Scout Guarding a Culvert

Hints to Night-watchers, Scouts, and Despatch Riders.
Some of the Danger Signs to Look Out for

Specially Described for THE SPHERE

The great secret of war is secrecy—silence is a good way of keeping a secret. The most wonderful of all scouts and despatch carriers are the North American Indians, and solely because of their silence and knowledge of woodlore.

Assuming that the scout or night watcher is capable of concealing his movements and actions there are many danger signs to look for which will materially help him, but I wish it to be clearly understood that these signs are purely woodlore and not in any way to do with military tactics.

There are many signs about the country-side which show, to those who know, the presence of men, and those signs come chiefly from the birds. A rook winging its way in the distance will suddenly wheel at right angles should it observe a man or men with guns. A bird is no fool and knows the uses to which a gun is put. Be wary if you see this occur.

A hawk beginning to stoop or fall will suddenly recover itself and appear to be violently interested in the distance to the horizon if it espies a man—be very careful. There is nothing more careful than a bird. It may be taken, however, as a sign of safety if you see the hawk stoop and complete the movement; there is nothing more there than perhaps a very desperate field mouse.

Blackbirds are useful tell-tales, but perhaps only for men who are dismounted and are scouting, and most of the signs I am telling you of are for the man at some distance away to see. A blackbird, should he be disturbed by a man or men creeping behind a hedge, will make a sudden dash and give a kind of running chatter while he is doing it. This chatter stops suddenly when the bird has got to cover again. Should you be riding down an apparently safe road at night and hear this chatter, it may be that you yourself have put the bird up, but should you be making a survey of the country, and see this occur some distance from you, be wary; it may, of course, only be a stoat prowling around, but again in time of war it may be men. Another point, if you do hear this chatter at night, is to switch off your light as you go by; the back glare from your lamp will make an excellent target after you have passed the danger mark should there be men at that spot.

Birds, and especially wood pigeons—a wood pigeon is about the shyest thing on wings—in wooded country on being alarmed—guns alarm wood pigeons most horribly—will suddenly rise up and circle above the tree tops and then settle again. Should they keep it up—i.e., rising circling, and settling—you can rely on it that there is something very strange indeed in that wood.

Be on your guard should you hear an owl hoot at night. Owls are extraordinary birds and hoot for various reasons. They may be hunting, but on the other hand it may be a warning note or just one of mere fright. If the bird is hunting all's well, but if it be a warning note all's not well; anyway you can see the difficulty you have to encounter. Be suspicious and

don't go near the direction from which the sound comes. An owl's hoot is about the easiest thing to imitate that there is and is extensively used as a warning note by scouts.

The lapwings' call is another. The sound they

Guarding a Railway Embankment and Culvert
Boy Scouts changing guard

make is "pee wit," which serves as another name for the lapwing.

Another sign useful for dismounted scouts is that rabbits on being alarmed—they post sentries around their warrens—will drum with their back

legs on the ground; it is quite astonishing to what a distance this sound will carry on a still night. I attach it to the fact that the numerous tunnels made by these small fellows act as a sort of drum. A good suggestion for scouts is to move as quietly as possible and make no sudden movements. A head bobbing up against the skyline would give your position away to a nicety, so move slowly and surely. Become dead still should anything attract you as suspicious, and wherever possible scout up against the wind. Those little chaps who will help you will then not hear or scent your approach. Remember another thing. These small animals can hear a great deal better than you can and have more advantage for doing so, especially from the one fact that they are so much nearer the ground than you are.

A good way of listening for the approach of anyone is to lay your ear, not on the ground, but close to it.

You may often hear on a still night the faint bark of some watchdog at a farm. This may mean anything, but you may depend on it that a dog barks at night for one reason only. Something or someone of a suspicious nature is moving about. Note the direction of this sound and if travelling towards it emulate the dog and be suspicious also. Should the bark suddenly end in a yelp or a yelp occur after the bark be doubly suspicious. In an enemy's country a barking dog will soon get acquainted with the business end of a bayonet.

Grass moving where there is no wind should make anyone suspicious. Many observers have commented on the lack of wild life in a country overrun with soldiery. A big battle acts as a sort of army of beaters and drives all wild things before it. You are certainly in a strange and suspicious country where there is no sign of wild life.

You may take it that a road is fairly safe at night if you observe ahead of you twin red lights. These red lights, needless to say, are the eyes of small night foragers intent on the same business as yourself, i.e., getting through the dangers of the night safely. These lights appear to be some distance above the level of the road and look like the back lamp of a car, but it is merely a night illusion. You may depend upon it that where these lights appear no man exists. To really recognise them they appear to stay for some little time dead still. The forager in question has seen your lamp and adapted his method of freezing. They carry this frozen attitude so far sometimes that you eventually blot them out, but generally those tell-tale lights are switched off with a suddenness that leaves you blinking. The animal has evaporated, as it were, in the way these small animals have. I am afraid that you will not find many roads like this.

If a despatch rider uses an electric light. To switch it off when danger threatens will leave your enemy in a very disconcerted plight, which is, of course, your main objective.

Boy Scouts on the Look-out for the Enemy
Creeping along under cover

Image © Illustrated London News Group

Training for unseen observation of the enemy. (The Sphere)

A despatch rider handing in his message. (The Sphere)

Boy Scouts usually playing a major role in this task. Not everyone was caught up by the belief that the Germans would attempt to poison the water supply. In Sussex a meeting of the Battle Urban District Council (UDC) discussed the guarding of the town's water supply. Although it was eventually decided to use Boy Scouts and others to guard the facilities there was some dissent with one councillor, Mr C. Sheppard, stating that the idea of German spies poisoning the water supply was 'one of the most absurd things ever thought of', and that the guarding of the facilities 'was entirely unnecessary'.[3] Twenty-five scouts from the Mansfield Troop were ferried by motor vehicle to a variety of vulnerable points where they mounted guard. The scouts in the Keighley area were particularly well organised; by 20 August they had mounted guard over the town's water and transport network. The 1st (Parish Church) Troop were guarding three nearby reservoirs, the 7th (St Ann's) Troop were guarding the Holme Mills culvert, the Oakworth Troop were performing a similar duty at the Corporation

Filter Beds and the 3rd (YMCA) Keighley Troop were in charge of guarding the local railway bridges. These guards were mounted day and night and there was a complete system of reliefs organised.

Such activities were taking place across Britain throughout the first weeks of the war. At the Boy Scouts' depot at Springhill, Burnley, the scouts prepared for their duties in guarding telegraph facilities by packing mattresses to act as sandbags and digging trenches to allow for easier defence of such sites.

To aid the Boy Scouts in their endeavours the local and national press carried articles which gave advice to those who were expected to be observant and to move quietly by night and day. Scouts were advised to take notice of natural signs. The activities of birds were especially useful to the scout. A blackbird's warning chatter, the hoot of an owl or the circling of wood pigeons were all signs that something may be amiss. Rabbits were also of use as they posted sentries outside their burrows. Other advice included the necessity to move slowly and to be conscious of one's surroundings at all times in order to avoid being

Scouts prepare mattresses and dig trenches at Springhill. (Burnley News)

spotted against, for example, the skyline. Dispatch-riders who used an electric light on their bicycle at night were advised to turn it off if they noted any suspicious activity.

This was all a wider part of the spy-mania which gripped the country in the early months of the war. Scouts were ordered to be on the look out for suspicious characters, especially if they were foreign. While this was worthwhile, it did at times backfire due to the febrile atmosphere in the country. Some scouts proved to be overly zealous and the police were inundated with reports of possible spies with many innocent people being detained, usually briefly, by the police. With their training encouraging them to be both good citizens and to show loyalty to King and country, the Boy Scouts were often those who were keenest lookouts for possible foreign spies. At Carmarthen in the first fortnight of the war three German men who were strangers in the town were arrested after a Boy Scout had observed one of the men loitering near to an 'important point'.[4] The boy immediately notified the police and provided a description which allowed the police to locate and arrest the man and to identify two others, whom they also detained.

Clay Cross Church Troop had an exciting beginning to the war. The boys were due to have a camp at Skegness but transport problems forced a cancellation and the scouts instead decamped to Cleethorpes where they were permitted to camp on the golf course. They were surrounded by soldiers from the Territorials who were guarding the town. After setting up their camp they quickly began to liaise with the soldiers and each boy served a four-hour night duty with the soldiers. All of which, claimed Scoutmaster Mr P. Wilcockson and his deputy Mr C. Steele-Perkins, was hugely beneficial to the boys. On the night of 12 August, the boys were ordered to douse their cooking fires and move their tents as the officer in charge feared that there might be German spies about. All of the boys immediately volunteered for night duty and the officer later commented that he was very pleased with how the scouts had followed the orders given to them. The experiences, claimed the leaders, made the boys realise that being scouts in 'time of war does not mean all play'.[5] A week after the excitement at their camp the boys from the Clay Cross Troop found themselves, at the request of the Chief Constable, maintaining a guard, consisting of Scoutmaster Wilcockson and seven scouts, over a reservoir at Tibshelf.

These quasi-military duties, while attracting widespread praise from the majority of the public, did also open the association up to certain allegations. The scouts were accused by some of having been 'unmasked, and proved to be, after all, a war movement'.[6] This was fervently denied by the association and its defenders who retorted that the scouts were being used in a non-military way and were employed mainly with the Red Cross, with agriculture and with aiding the civil authorities. Others saw nothing wrong with the Boy Scouts being used in a military capacity and there were a number of articles which praised the boys for showing that they possessed a sense of masculinity. Typical of these was the caption used in a photograph published in the *Illustrated London News* on 22 August, which showed scouts guarding a railway tunnel at Andover with the caption stating: 'Youngsters who have proved themselves men!'[7]

Many Boy Scout troops were on their summer camps when war was announced. Among these were the Southampton District Association. The scouts were encamped at Alum Bay and, with war announced, were able to give aid to the native Freshwater Troop, who had been ordered by the military authorities to make a house-to-house inspection of the area in order to identify any aliens who were living there. Other Southampton troops were employed on the docks, mainly in guiding soldiers. Altogether, some fifty or so Southampton scouts were involved in dock work. They were drawn mainly from the 1st, 2nd, 11th and 20th Troops. In addition to these duties, the scouts from Southampton were employed in guard duties, in conveying messages for the police in rural areas, while some of the older boys were being employed in aiding the various ladies' committees which had sprung up to provide aid to the troops. These boys were used to purchase items, to help publicise the various groups, and to prepare splints and bandages.

Scouts guard tunnel at Andover. (Illustrated London News)

The more specialised Sea Scouts also volunteered their services with the Chief Scout offering the Admiralty the use of 1,000 scouts to guard coastlines in whatever way was required. The London Sea Scouts were quickly dispatched to a number of coastguard stations on the coast of Kent to render assistance to the coastguards. Among the Sea Scouts who undertook this duty was the Troop from the *Daily Mirror*, on 7 August a patrol of eight senior scouts was sent to the coastguard station at Ramsgate. The boys quickly set up their tent and organised their cooking equipment and by midnight they were patrolling the cliffs in pairs. Their reception from the coastguard was welcoming, with the men describing the scouts as 'fine big fellows'.[8] The Ramsgate detachment was led by 17-year-old P.L. Ernest Snowdon who, although the youngest member, stood at 6ft 2in. Two more patrols from the Daily Mirror Troop were also active by this time. This was despite the fact that almost half of the Daily Mirror Troop had enlisted in the regular forces. One was sent to aid the coastguards at Dover while the other was at Herne Bay assisting the St Agatha's Troop in patrolling the coast and roads and in guarding telegram and telephone lines and the local railway network. The Kensington 'North Pole' Troop were stationed at Reculver, three patrols from the Toynbee Troop were at Hythe, the Marquis of Northampton's Own were at Dover, the 9th Greenwich at Walmer, the 1st Deptford at Littlestone, the 2nd Kingston at Dungeness and a mixed patrol was stationed at Sandwich.

Scouts were used for such duties up and down the east coast, as well as in aiding the military units which were guarding the coast. In Northumberland, Admiral Startin inspected the Lowick Boy Scouts who were stationed at Bamburgh in early September. The Admiral complimented the boys on their presentation and went on to say that even though they were far from home, the experience of day and night duty was wonderful training for them and would be of great benefit in future years.

The claims that the scouts were not being used in a military capacity was not always true. With the Territorials called up and encamped across Britain many scouts found themselves aiding the 'Terriers'. For the majority who found themselves undertaking such duties, their role consisted largely of helping in the cookhouse and other non-combat roles. Despite this menial role, the scouts who found themselves alongside the Territorials were delighted at being asked to help these volunteer soldiers.

Elsewhere, patriotic Boy Scouts took part in urging young men to volunteer for service to King and country. The methods used to encourage volunteers ranged from the purely patriotic encouragement to the coercive. In Birmingham the scouts had their band parading through the streets acting as an unofficial recruiting agency which urged patriotic young men to follow them to the recruiting station at Suffolk Street.

The troops were ordered to redouble their efforts with more regular meetings to be held and a focus placed upon scouts earning their ambulance, missioner, pathfinder, fireman, handyman, signaller,

Scouts peeling potatoes at the Platt Fields camp of a Territorial unit of the Royal Artillery. (Manchester Evening News)

Birmingham scouts band on a recruiting drive. (Evening Dispatch)

telegraphist, cook and gardener badges so that they could provide the most valuable assistance to the authorities as possible. Boys aged 11–18 were urged to join the scouts so that they could learn useful skills and former members were urged to re-join their troops.

One of the more unusual and dangerous tasks entrusted to some Boy Scouts during the first weeks of the war was that of giving aid to British residents stranded abroad. On 21 August the *Manchester Evening News* gave the account of one such boy.

Despatched on 13 August to locate, deliver money to, and aid the return of a group of ladies who had become stranded near Vichy in France, he had endured many discomforts on his travels to France. Once there he related how he had slowly made his way to Vichy despite many hardships. The train ride from Boulogne to Paris had taken over nine hours and when near to Paris he had been illuminated by a searchlight which had left him somewhat disconcerted. In Paris the Boy Scout ran into difficulties in obtaining travel papers, but he was aided by an Englishman he had met on the way to France who spoke more French than he did. While in Paris he was mistaken for a Russian sailor, a British sailor, a Highlander, and a German. Eventually securing a place on a train bound for St Germain-les-Fosses, he set off again upon his mission. This train journey was even longer, taking over eleven hours, but was enlivened for him by the sight of many troops, including a troop train full of African Zouaves. Upon arrival he encountered an English boy who directed him to a train bound for Vichy. One can imagine his disappointment when he arrived at Vichy only to be told, by what he described as a very unhelpful hotel porter, that the ladies had set out the day before for an unknown destination.

Deciding that his only course of action was to return home, he met with yet more paperwork difficulties and was helped by a French Boy Scout. Having been delayed by a day, the following day was Sunday so, like a good Boy Scout, he attended church where he met and lunched with a group of English people. During the Sunday he was escorted by the Senior Patrol Leader from Vichy, who he described as being most interested in the English Boy Scouts and who explained that all French scouts were in government employ now. The return train journey to Paris took fourteen hours and this was followed by another long journey to Boulogne.

In Boulogne the exhausted scout had to wait for the boat and met with two Privates from the Royal Army Service Corps (RASC) who showed him the facilities of their field kitchen. The two men were going home on leave and he accompanied them onto the boat before making arrangements for one of them to have a bath (neither of the soldiers spoke good French). The boat contained a large number of aliens coming to England and he described how each one had to fill in forms before being allowed to board. Finally, he arrived back in England on 18 August after an exciting five-day odyssey. The final part of his journey was concluded when he drove to his headquarters and returned the money that had been entrusted to him.

This was one of many such adventures undertaken by Boy Scouts during the chaotic early days of the war. That the boys were trusted with such tasks underlines just how much faith many in authority had in them, but also betrays a certain lack of care for their wellbeing in sending inexperienced boys out into a dangerous wartime situation.

On 19 September there was a grand occasion for the scouts of Portsmouth. On the Saturday afternoon a large parade drawn from all of the Portsmouth Troops was drawn up and inspected by Brigadier General Kelly, the commanding officer of the Royal Garrison Artillery (RGA), Southern Coast Defences. Present at the parade among other dignitaries were the District Scout Commissioner (Lieutenant Colonel Clinton Holloway) and the Assistant Commissioner (Dr Aldous). The reason for the parade and ceremony was the award of the bronze medal and certificate of the Royal Humane Society to Patrol Leader A. Lander (13) of the 31st (Warblington Street) Troop. On 4 July, Lander had gone to the aid of a boy who had gotten into trouble in the water, despite risk to his own life. Having pulled the boy from the water, Lander then gave resuscitation for an hour and had succeeded in saving the boy's life.

Presenting the medal, General Kelly praised the scout movement in general, claiming that it was the skills and principles for good instilled into Lander which had enabled him to perform his deeds. General Kelly also praised the scouts who had come under his command at the beginning of the war, saying that they had conducted themselves well and had been of great use.

Not everyone was a supporter of the activities of the scouts during these early weeks of war. One correspondent wrote to *The Bystander* at the end of September that the Boy Scouts Association had now become an anti-militaristic group which gave young men the chance to shirk their military duty to join up by instead offering some form of non-military service. The correspondent was especially scathing about the ex-scouts of military age who had re-joined the association and those scoutmasters who were of military age but had failed to join up. The correspondent alleged that the majority of scoutmasters were fit young men aged 17–30 and that they were thus the exact men who should be joining Kitchener's Army. The paper refuted the assertions of the correspondent by stating that in many cases such men had proven unfit for military duty, often through lack of height, while in others they were the breadwinner for a family who would be rendered destitute if they left behind their work. In other words, the paper was saying that not every man of military age was suitable for service and that the scouts provided a good way of still serving the country in this case. In many cases this was true and the number of scoutmasters who had in fact joined up was very high.

We have already heard how the scouts were giving assistance to the various groups that were offering comforts for the troops. In Glasgow the scouts had even set up their own effort and were touring the streets asking for donations of reading materials such as books, magazines and periodicals which would be donated to soldiers and sailors. The scheme was highly successful and was just one example of how even younger members could make an active contribution to the war effort.

When war was declared there had been a party of French Scouts present in the Portsmouth area and they had been unable to return to

Glasgow Boy Scouts collecting reading materials for soldiers and sailors. (Daily Record)

their own country until mobilisation had been completed. The French scouts had joined in with the local scouts in undertaking patrols of the coast and other vital points in order to help the British Army but by early October they had been granted permission to return to their own country. On Saturday 10 October, therefore, a large parade took place on Grosvenor's Green to pay farewell to the French visitors. The District Commissioner, Lieutenant Colonel Clinton Holloway, described the event as possibly being unique in that, to his knowledge, no foreign scouts had ever before combined to help defend the country. To mark this special occasion the Portsmouth Association presented the French scoutmaster and each of his lads with a special commemorative 'Thanks' badge. The Portsmouth Association had also applied for affiliation with their French visitors. Scoutmaster Harvey, the French scoutmaster, expressed his thanks and appreciation that they had played a part in the defence of the British coast before stating that he believed that everyone saw the British scout movement as being the ideal of boyhood.

The continued use of scouts in aiding the civil and military authorities proved to be one which was contentious in some areas. Boys being used in this manner were often not attending school and it was felt that not only might their education be adversely affected, but that local authorities often had a difficult enough job in sending their children to school without this added excuse. Different councils reacted in different ways; many were prepared to excuse scouts attending school if it was confirmed that they were undertaking urgent duties which were of help to the war effort, while others remained more circumspect. Towards the end of October 1914, the Education Committee of Reigate Council met to discuss the problem. It was agreed that there would be three recommendations. These forbade any Boy Scout under the age of 12 being allowed to absent himself from school, that no Boy Scout or member of such an organisation would be permitted to absent himself from school to undertake work at a horse depot, and that no Boy Scout be allowed to absent himself from school to undertake public service unless under urgent and special circumstances, and then only with official permission. Clearly this meant that the Boy Scouts would only be of use in an emergency or at weekends and there was a marked reluctance to allow school-age scouts to take part in such work. Indeed, the chairman of the committee admitted that the very next day the local association had written to him to reassure him that no school-age scouts were currently employed. It was admitted that the boys had performed a useful function immediately after declaration of war, but that their education was also important and must not be neglected. Some reassurances were given that if an emergency did arise, then the magistrates would be lenient in the case of Boy Scouts who had absented themselves to help out.

Throughout the autumn and winter of 1914 Sir Robert Baden-Powell attempted to alert people to the possibility of German raids upon coastal towns. The Chief Scout urged maximum vigilance and exhorted scouts on coastguard duties not to let their guard down for an instant. By November he was going further, claiming that an invasion could also be possible with the German navy being able to assemble up to 90,000 men in transports and land at some unopposed, out-of-the-way spot. Baden-Powell asserted that, contrary to many, such an invasion force would probably not land on the more populated south coast but would attempt to land on the east coast, most likely Yorkshire. His logic for this was based upon a captured German document which claimed that London was merely the administrative centre of Britain but that the key areas were the industrial towns and cities of the north. Such an attack would be able to quickly capture and destroy much of this industry and leave Britain unable to carry on with the war. One of the places where Sir Robert delivered this message was Hartlepool, where he addressed a gathering of scouts on 12 December.

On the morning of 16 December a German flotilla managed to breach the coastal defences off the north-east coast and bombard the towns of Hartlepool, Scarborough and Whitby, killing 137 people and injuring some 592. Among the casualties was a young scout named Miller who had to have his leg amputated. The young lad was buoyed by a message of appreciation which he received from Sir Robert Baden-Powell.

By the end of the year the scouts had more than proven their value to the authorities and came in for much praise. In 1914 there were some 200,000 scouts and cubs in Britain and half of these had been employed in public service during this first year of war.

With increased recruitment meaning that the scouts were stood down from the quasi-military duties, such as guarding railway lines, that they had undertaken at the start of the war there was a freeing up of trained and eager boys. Many of these scouts were instead transferred to working for various government departments (both national and local government) where they immediately proved very useful. These scouts undertook tasks such as being employed as orderlies and dispatch-riders. In London, the 100 scouts who had initially been assigned to duties at the War Office were bolstered by hefty reinforcement and so large did the force become that a scoutmaster from North London was placed in charge of the boys. The majority of these boys were assigned duties which had them running about the building at every hour of day or night carrying important telegrams and memos. A smaller number, under the command of an assistant scoutmaster, dealt with messages which had to be taken to other locations and utilised bikes and motor vehicles for these duties.

The scoutmaster in charge of the boys at the War Office gave them high praise, describing how they set about every task put to them with enthusiasm and vigour, fully aware of the vital importance of the job to which they had been assigned. This praise was reflected by the War Office itself with the department arranging for every boy to receive a week's holiday after every three months of service. When the funeral of Field Marshal Frederick Sleigh Roberts, 1st Earl Roberts, VC, KG, KP, GCB, OM, GCSI, GCIE, KStJ, VD, PC, FRSGS, took place at St Paul's Cathedral in November, the War Office requested that a detachment of Boy Scouts from the War Office be present.

Given the increasing susceptibility of Britain to either invasion or raiding, and the growing spy-mania, it was perhaps understandable that many within the movement wished for a more active role. In the November issue of the Boy Scouts Association's journal, the *Headquarters Gazette*, Robert Baden-Powell informed the movement of his intent to inaugurate a Scouts Defence Corps. In the article he declared that in the event of an invasion a 16-year-old boy who had been trained in musketry would be of more value to the country than a dozen men who were completely untrained, and that every scout aged 15–17 should be encouraged to put his name forward via his scoutmaster as being willing to serve in the event of an emergency.

Baden-Powell was keenly aware that this development would immediately arouse the ire of those who had already criticised the scout movement as being overtly militant in nature. He argued that membership in the corps was purely voluntary, was not a permanent feature of the movement, being a measure put in place for the duration of the war only, and was, instead of a militant move, a part of the struggle against militarism. Baden-Powell was keenly aware that the country's situation was dangerous and that many young scouts were eager to play their part militarily in the event of an emergency such as an invasion. In order to promote the corps he wrote to every scout district and to the press encouraging a large and positive response to the initiative. Sir Robert declared that there could be no harm in helping the older boys of the scouts to prepare to defend their homes if it proved necessary.

The terms and conditions attached to membership in the Scouts Defence Corps made it clear that no scout of military service age could apply, and all applicants had to have written permission from their parents or guardians. Other terms, however, gave the lie to the claim that it was not a military initiative. Among other regulations they explained how the scouts involved were to be trained primarily as infantry, although a small number could be trained as cycle troops (largely to be used as dispatch riders), cavalry or even seamen (in the case of the sea scouts).

The proposed organisation of the corps also reflected a military bent. Baden-Powell declared that patrols of eight could be termed a section and formed into platoons, with four platoons forming a company and four companies a battalion, which would be under the command of a commissioner (each battalion would therefore consist of 512 scouts, not including officers).

Writing to district commissioners across Britain, Baden-Powell stated that it had been intimated to him by the authorities that if the current stalemate on the Western Front continued, there was a belief that Germany might attempt to knock Britain out of the war by an invasion or repeated raiding. With the regular army abroad and the majority of recruits being required to bolster this force, any man who could be trained in the defence of Britain was a valuable commodity. He argued that if the scouts could, in the event of an enemy landing, provide several thousand lads trained in military discipline, rudimentary tactics and marksmanship, then it might tip the balance in the country's favour.

Once again, however, Baden-Powell was eager to explain that this was purely a temporary wartime measure, would not become a regular part of the movement and that Britain's part in the current war was siding against militarism. The Chief Scout went on to explain,

> We are driven to be on our defence lest we come under the heel of the Prussian bully, and it is the duty of every patriot who has sufficient strength, to take up arms in a just cause, with no feeling of aggression or blood-thirstiness, but solely for the protection of his country and his kind in the hour of danger.[9]

The second thrust of Baden-Powell's argument in favour of the Scouts Defence Corps was that of training. He argued that although at the present moment only men of 19 or over, and of sufficiently good stature, were being accepted into the forces, that could very soon change, with smaller men being accepted and even, as was happening in Germany and other nations, lads of 16 or over (at least for home service). If this did happen then, he argued, it was the duty of everyone to be prepared. As Chief Scout he said: 'I want all Scouts to Be Prepared for this and to have our "Scouts Defence Corps" ready, so that the moment the door is opened, we can step in with a corps trained and ready for service.)[10]

The commissioners and scoutmasters would have a leading role in promoting the new corps. Baden-Powell urged them to encourage every scout of the correct age group to put their name forward; to quickly organise these boys into patrols for the purpose of self-training and that training should immediately commence, focusing on rifle shooting, judging distance, signalling, pioneering, entrenching, drilling in accordance with army infantry training, scouting, first-aid, and camp cooking. Much of this training could take place in the evenings with patrol leaders appointed at first on a probationary basis so that the best could be sought. The Chief Scout also encouraged the commissioners and local associations to secure the help of miniature rifle ranges if possible and to try to recruit instructors from the ranks of old sportsmen, gamekeepers and the like.

Across Britain, local associations responded immediately and with enthusiasm. To many who were involved with the movement, this was the moment they had been waiting for since war had been declared, and, within days of the appeal from the Chief Scout, local associations were forming their own defence corps. Associations moved speedily. The Aberdeen association was particularly quick off the mark, holding the first parade of its new defence corps on Saturday 28 November. The association was encouraged by the number of volunteers who had come forward and, after the parade, the various sections, patrols, and platoons were provisionally organised. A meeting of scoutmasters was arranged at Leeds on 30 November to discuss the formation of the local Scouts Defence Corps. On 5 December a meeting of the officers of the Stockport and District Association was convened to discuss the formation of a defence corps. Enthusiasm was evident from the fact that there were over fifty attendees. The district commissioner explained the details of the scheme, adding that every volunteer would have his own equipment and be expected to be ready at a moment's notice. He also added the assurance that this scheme 'in no way alters the non-military training of the movement, being in fact, an emergency preparation for an emergency'.[11] After the scheme had been discussed at length, a motion was put forward that the scheme be adopted and that a local defence corps battalion be formed. This motion was overwhelmingly carried with only two dissenting. At Portsmouth, the association could report on 18 December that matters were well in hand and that satisfactory progress was being made, aided by the influence of the services and by the large number of scouts and 'old boys' who had volunteered their time.[12]

Military Service

The early scouting organisation was highly influenced by militaristic thinking. It emphasised duty, loyalty, fair-play and chivalrous behaviour, and good citizenship alongside the physical activities, many of which were applicable in military organisations. This is unsurprising given the origin of the movement. Lieutenant General Robert Baden-Powell's book had found fame as the defender of the town of Mafeking during the Second Boer War and in the skills of scouting he utilised a variety of games and contests that he had used in his training of cavalry troops. He had also been impressed by the field-skill abilities of the Boer Commandos against whom he had fought. He used these experiences to write a book entitled *Scouting for Boys*, published in 1908. The book was originally intended to be applied by organisations which were already in existence, such as the Boys' Brigade, but such was its popularity that Scout Troops were quickly organised.

Given the nature of scouting, with its emphasis on loyalty to King and country, duty and the manliness of military-style skills, it is hardly surprising that many men associated with the movement found themselves on the frontlines in the very first days and weeks of the war. Many were members of the regular army or were reserves who had formerly served and were recalled immediately or were members of the Territorials.

At 11 am on the morning of Sunday 16 August, a large number of boys from the Hampshire District Association were drawn up on parade. The occasion was to pay farewell to members and former members who had been called up. The parade was held in front of St Mark's Anglican Church and, besides the scouts, was attended by members of the local army units. A semi-military service was held during which the current war was compared to that between good and evil, and both scouts and soldiers were urged to remain strong in their faith in both God and King and country. Following the service, communion was held for those who had been called up and they were showered with good wishes from the scouts.

With the war just weeks old, the former County Scout Commissioner for Banffshire was killed in action while serving with 1 Gordon Highlanders (he was a member of the 3rd Battalion but was serving on attachment). Captain Lachlan Gordon-Duff of Drummuir and Park House, Cornhill, Banffshire, was a married man aged 34 when he was killed on 24 October.[13] As the fighting continued there were several more scouts killed in action. Private Roland James Walker had been a member of the scouts in Eastbourne and enlisted in 1 Queen's Own (Royal West Kent Regiment); he was killed, aged just 18, on 30 October.[14]

Just one day after the death of Captain Gordon-Duff, another notable former scout was killed in action. Many men who had moved from Britain to one of the colonies for work threw themselves into the Boy Scouts movement. Many of these men travelled back to Britain to enlist at the beginning of the war. Among them was Sergeant Edward Charters White (32) who joined 2 Black Watch and was killed on 31 October. Sergeant White was a native of Clapham but had moved to India where he had been assistant scoutmaster of the scout Troop at Fort William, Calcutta.[15]

By the end of November it was believed that 10,000 ex-scouts and scoutmasters had joined up. This was a remarkable record, given that many of these men could quite easily have avoided service if they wished at this stage of the war.

December brought the deaths of yet more former scouts. Lance Corporal Arthur Daphne (22) had been assistant scoutmaster to the 5th North London Troop and had joined 5 London's (London Rifle Brigade) as a private. On 13 December he was shot and killed while trying to aid an injured comrade. Arthur was from a family of lawyers and barristers. His late father, Pasco, had been a barrister and both his older brothers, Frank and Maurice, had also joined the profession, being located at 71 Lincoln's Inn Fields. It would appear that Arthur, however, had not followed the family tradition and had instead found employment as an accountant. The pride that his family had in Arthur is evident in the wording of the death notification that they placed in the press. It read, in part, 'He was shot while trying to bring a wounded friend out of danger. "Greater love hath no man than this".'[16]

One of the foremost members of the organisation to be killed in this first year of the war was Captain Sir Montague Aubrey Rowley Cholmeley, of Easton Hall, Grantham, Lincolnshire. A keen huntsman, he was Master of the Burton Hunt, Sir Montague was the Scout Commissioner for Lincolnshire and, before leaving for service with 2 Grenadier Guards, he had written to the local scouts telling them:

> Scouts of Lincolnshire, I have the good fortune to be going to-day where I know you would all wish to be. In saying farewell, I leave you to uphold all the splendid traditions of the Scouts. Any small service I have rendered, you can best repay by responding loyally to your country's call.

Sir Montague was killed in action on Christmas Eve and his body was never recovered. Days later a wounded member of his company told the *Lincolnshire Echo* how his Captain had died. The battalion had been in action the day before Christmas Eve and had captured a length of German trench. On Christmas Eve the Germans mounted a counter-attack and by 9 am they were throwing grenades into the trench occupied by the company. The guardsman related how Sir Montague had walked along the trench telling his men to keep their heads down when a grenade exploded next to him and he was hit in the head and killed. The attack was so fierce that the battalion was driven from its position and forced to abandon its dead.[17]

Brought up in a spirit of duty to King and country, it is no surprise that many former scouts had been among the immediate rush to join the colours in the first days of the war. Among them was Harry Leslie Caulder. After being educated at Weybridge School, where he had won numerous trophies for shooting with the Weybridge Rifle Club, he had obtained a job in the audit department of South Western Railways aged just 15. He had worked there for five years when he joined up two days after war was declared. Posted to the 14 London Regiment (London Scottish), he had written home to his parents at their home at 'Kelpie', Springfield Meadows, Weybridge, describing the first two actions he had been in. He had sustained a slight wound to the knee in the second, but on 19 December he had taken part in another action and had been

Above left: *(l-r) Lady Cholmeley,*
Mr Swan and Sir Montague Cholmeley.
(The Tatler)

Above right: *Lady Cholmeley and*
daughter. (The Sphere)

Right: *Captain Sir Montague Aubrey*
Rowley Cholmeley. (Illustrated
Sporting & Dramatic News)

seriously wounded. His parents were notified that Private Caulder had succumbed to his wounds on 26 December. It was reported in some quarters that Private Caulder, despite having been badly wounded, had gone out from his trench and successfully brought back a wounded comrade.[18]

CHAPTER 2

1915

The Home Front

The boy scouts earned a great deal of praise for their willingness to help out in the local community and with so many active charities, their help was needed. At Tayport, the National Relief Fund obtained a box of gifts which had been sent from America and arrived shortly before the New Year. The main problem was how to distribute these gifts at this time of year, but the local scouts eagerly offered their aid and quickly delivered the gifts to their recipients.

Early in 1915 the 13th Hussars had been sent to France and a little later the Commander in Chief of Allied Forces, Sir John French, invited Sir Robert Baden-Powell, as Honorary Colonel of the regiment, to visit them in France. Baden-Powell duly did so and during his visit he was struck by the importance of the few YMCA recreation huts which had been set up for the soldiers.

Some parts of the country were better provided with scout and sea scout troops than others. In Northumberland, for example, there was no shortage of enthusiasm, but the local movement was rather disorganised and some parts of the large county were lacking in sufficient numbers. On 15 January the 1st Withington (59th Manchester) Troop was asked to provide reinforcements to provide a coastguard at Newbiggin. The boys set off on 18 January and, after enduring a five-hour train journey, arrived to no welcome. They knew the location of their quarters, however, and began their tramp across the damp sand, arriving at their quarters to find it locked up and empty. Using their initiative, the sea scouts assessed their supplies and started a fire in the watch house. They used the fire to boil up some Oxo cubes and, with some bread, this sufficed as their meal. After they had been supplied with the key to their quarters they quickly settled in and cleaned them up before undertaking their duties. These boys remained on this duty for the next six months and upon their return to their homes won praise for their physical development during this time.

During their time in Newbiggin the sea scouts from Manchester won widespread praise, not only for performing their duties as coastguards, but also for their willingness to help out in the local community. The boys had many interesting experiences during their six months in Northumberland. One of the highlights for the boys was the sighting and reporting of two Zeppelins crossing the coast on a bombing mission. They also witnessed a steamer being torpedoed and sunk. Their time in Northumberland was marked by poor weather and they found much wreckage strewn along the coast when they patrolled. They also witnessed the sinking of a fishing boat and of two fishing cobles which were sunk in a blizzard with the loss of seven lives. During this gale the sea scouts were unable to access fresh water and so they resorted to melting snow for their drinking and washing water.

All around the country scouts and sea scouts were carrying out such duties in coastal communities. The boys and their parents were often left impressed when the lads returned home as to how the often harsh duties upon which they had been employed had helped their physical development, and many were the comments upon how a somewhat scrawny lad had gone away and a muscular and fit scout had returned. The coastal communities themselves often benefited as the scouts fulfilled their duty to help others on a regular basis. This led to scouts throwing themselves into voluntary efforts to help the communities in a wide variety of ways while learning new skills themselves.

We have already seen how the scouts were assisting the War Office, but it was not only in running messages and dispatches that the scouts made a contribution. Across the whole country ad-hoc military camps were being hastily constructed to cope with the massive influx of men who would make up Kitchener's New Army. Labour shortages, however, were a constant issue and the War Office often needed assistance to complete these essential tasks in the time given. At Birmingham, the War Office asked for help in the erecting of huts and stables and the assistance of 200 local boy scouts was gratefully accepted.

Birmingham Boy Scouts at work erecting a row of stables. (Illustrated Sporting and Dramatic News)

The popularity of the Boy Scouts Defence Corps had been such that many younger boys had petitioned to be allowed to join and the opening weeks of 1915 saw the age limit reduced from 14 to 15. The activities of the corps were of such interest that the boys involved that they would brave harsh weather to attend. A snowstorm in Aberdeen in January did not prevent an encouraging attendance at a meeting of the corps held in the city; it was hoped that the meeting to be held the following week would allow some outdoor activities and that the newly accepted 14-year-old volunteers would further swell the attendance.

Reaction to the recently announced formation of a Scouts Defence Corps was, as we have seen, very positive with both officers and scouts reacting with great enthusiasm. Further encouragement to scouts of an eligible age was that all who passed through their course of training in the Scouts Defence Corps would be 'allowed to reckon fourteen days towards their war services badge and rifles and ammunition [would] be issued to units when approved'.[1]

The setting up and training of such a force as the Scouts Defence Corps could not be completed overnight and it was acknowledged that the force would not be properly organised and trained for some time. Regardless, progress in many areas was well underway by mid-January. In Leeds, for example, the parental consent forms had already been sent out and the training of 'Boy Scout Bantams' had already begun in the central and north-east parts of the city with an indoor parade scheduled for the end of the month.[2]

The introduction of the Military Service Act in January 1916 meant that conscription was introduced in Britain. For many months in 1915 the government had made it plain that conscription was to be brought in and the effect of this impending change of policy upon the Scouts Defence Corps and the overall value of scouting in general was carefully considered by the officers of the association. The system of conscription which was proposed was quite complex and was a double-edged sword for the Scouts Defence Corps. Mass conscription would, on the one hand, deprive the corps of one of its functions as a feeder stream for the army, but on the other hand it helped, in the short term, to silence those who had objected to this militaristic development in the movement. After all, if any man of military age was to be called to serve, it could only be a good thing if there was a voluntary organisation in which men could learn some of the preliminary skills of soldiering before they were called up.

Aberdeen Boy Scouts Association was proud of the fact that it was the first in Scotland to form a Defence Corps. It was closely followed by the Dundee Association. Those boys who joined were warned that the first motto on the east coast must be 'Be Prepared', and that, having shown what they could do when mounting guard, people were reassured that they would 'again be of value' if an emergency did occur. Having been the first Scottish Defence Corps the Aberdonian boys were determined to also be the most efficient and quickly undertook a number of exercises such as route marches, lectures and drill. The boys were encouraged to learn as much as they could by observing the soldiers who were a common sight on the streets of the city. The boys were particularly exhorted to note 'the smart way in which the men salute officers whom they meet'.[3]

The enthusiasm for the Scouts Defence Corps seems to have been particularly buoyant in Scotland. We have already seen the early reaction in Aberdeen, but this was closely followed by several other local associations. In Dundee, it was hoped that a full battalion of 512 scouts between the ages of 14 and 17 would be raised. One of the first issues to be resolved when organising the corps was to provide suitable officers for the various units. The situation was often exacerbated by the fact that the most eligible and skilled men were either already serving, or were likely to enlist soon. The Dundee association had already appointed a commanding officer, Captain H.K. Smith (the county commissioner), and adjutant, Mr A. Lindsay Edwards (the county secretary), and a quartermaster, Mr K. Stuart Hall (the eastern secretary). By early January, however, the news had been received that a replacement quartermaster must be sought as

Mr Hall was shortly to take up a commission in the Northumberland Fusiliers.

Although enthusiasm for the Scouts Defence Corps was high among the officers and scouts there were problems in some areas. In Rugby there had been considerable concern expressed by the parents of scouts who wished to volunteer and a marked reluctance to sign the required permission slip. In an effort to alleviate these concerns the local association explained the reasoning behind the corps in the local press, but also subtly urged concerned parents to be more patriotic. The article in the *Rugby Advertiser*, written by Scoutmaster W.A. Randles of the 5th Rugby Troop, urged concerned parents to 'Remember the scouts of Belgium, who stood up with their fathers and elder brothers and did a man's share of the work.' And to also remember the example of 'our own scouts who remained at their posts during the Scarborough raid'. 'Were the people of Rugby,' he asked, 'to be less ready to prepare ourselves, and when prepared, to do our duty?' Once again, hoping to shame parents into giving way, he added that they all hoped that Britain would not be devastated like Belgium and France had been but 'if such an event comes to pass, and the Germans we may be sure will *try* to do so, we must be ready'. He concluded by saying that it was the duty of British people to prepare themselves, whether the Germans came or not, before telling parents: 'If your boys wish to train themselves, we ask you to give them your written consent to do so. They will not be compelled to do anything or go anywhere, but let us have them ready if they should be needed. Remember Louvain!'[4] The final rallying cry alluded to the sacking, looting and burning of the town of Louvain by German troops at the end of August 1914 when approximately 300 civilians were executed.[5]

The campaign to get the parents of boy scouts in Rugby to allow their sons to join the local Scouts Defence Corps seems to have borne fruit because a drill parade was arranged for 13 February at the Drill Hall. Events were also being organised to support the corps. A dance was to take place on the day before the parade and, with the movement being unable to solicit subscriptions without giving value for money, the organisers were keen to assure people that 'for 2s 6d they can have one of the best evening's pleasure they have ever experienced', and confirm that uniformed soldiers would be admitted free.[6] The organiser urged all sympathisers of the scout movement and patriotic people to attend if possible.

With the Scouts Defence Corps also maintaining its popularity among older boys it is unsurprising that there was an expansion into the aerial field. With the new aerial warfare being publicised in the press and attracting a certain glamour when compared to trench warfare it was only natural that many scouts wished to enter service in either the RFC or the RNAS. As a result, aviation classes were set up using instructors from the War Office. These classes trained boys who were approaching military service age in fitting and servicing aircraft and in preliminary knowledge of the service of the RFC. These classes proved highly popular and by the end of the year there were nine Air Schools for Boy Scouts operating in Britain.

The popularity of the Scouts Defence Corps was by no means universal and in some places it caused a split in local associations as those opposed to the increasing militarisation of the movement rebelled against those who claimed it was the patriotic duty of every scout of suitable age to serve in the force. At Burnley this rift was driven by the opposition of the majority of the local scoutmasters to the corps. In a letter to the local press at the end of January a scoutmaster who signed himself 'Parentis' complained of how two scoutmasters had gone against the vote of the local association at which the creation of defence corps was opposed by twenty-four votes to four. Parentis argued that Baden-Powell had stated that requests to join had to come through the scoutmasters, while others argued that permission of the parents was all that was needed. This confusion had led to some boys going against the wishes of their own scoutmaster (some of whom had promised that their scouts would not be used in military service), an act contrary to the Scout Law. Parentis himself did not actively oppose the corps, but was dismayed by the split that was occurring – and by the disobedience which the split was encouraging.

At the heart of these issues was the ambivalent nature of the corps. Clearly, in retrospect, the corps was a militarisation of the association but the fact that officers sought to distance the corps from the association muddied the waters and caused confusion. The argument in their favour was that boys in the defence corps were organised separately from the troops and patrols of the local associations, but this was at best a tenuous argument and one can understand the reluctance of some scoutmasters, many of whom viewed themselves as being in loco parentis when in charge of their scouts, and parents to see young boys, in some cases aged from just 14, joining what could be viewed as a military organisation.

The many Scouts Defence Corps units that were training all over the country by this point in the war were often bolstered by being inspected by a serving military officer. Such inspections gave great encouragement to the boys and made them feel that they were an accepted part of the military contribution to the war effort. Colonel Mitchell, the commanding officer of the Reserve battalion of 5 Yorks and Lancashire Regiment, carried out just such an inspection at Rotherham on 15 February 1915. There was an excellent muster of volunteers and, after the inspection, Colonel Mitchell emphasised the need for good discipline, punctuality and cleanliness, before praising the scouts for the number of relevant badges they were securing. The unit, in addition to the usual infantry, also possessed a small ambulance section. Four or five of the scouts had already possessed the ambulance badge and a further nine had gained the badge since the formation of the unit. The district chairman, Mr W. Dyson, explained to the colonel that added impetus had been given to the unit by the success of a scout named Roberts who had recently won the Donegal Badge for shooting. He also went on to detail how the local association had lost twelve scoutmasters and assistants who were by then on regular service and that there were also a number of 16-year-old scouts with the colours.

Demonstrating how the Scouts Defence Corps could be viewed with some ambivalence, however, he also opined that 'the corps was no part of the scout movement but was simply a temporary arrangement during the war'.[7]

Such an argument, and it was one which was frequently expressed, was not tenable. Clearly, the Scouts Defence Corps was fully intended to be a military force if mobilised. Even without mobilisation, the force was military in nature given the emphasis of the training given and was preparing boys of a suitable age for future military service.[8]

Although the scouts were well schooled in sensible behaviour they were still boys and the excitement of the war could often affect them as any other boy, sometimes with unfortunate consequences. Towards the end of March 1915, one boy scout from Bromley in Kent became a victim of his own curiosity. The scout, named Pavitt, had been walking close to a recently established Red Cross hospital when he saw a discarded cartridge lying on the ground. Curiosity got the better of the lad and he picked it up only for it to explode in his hand. The explosion tore his coat to shreds and left a part of the bullet embedded in a book he was carrying. Pavitt suffered facial injuries. It was determined that the cartridge was a German exploding cartridge and had probably been brought over by a wounded soldier as a souvenir.

Although the majority of Boy Scouts heeded the lessons of duty, honour and good behaviour, there were some who fell victim to letting youthful aggression get the better of them. In April a scout from Ashton, Manchester, was charged with having attacked another scout with a knife. John Hall (14) of 27 Bradgate Street was walking home from a scouts' meeting when he got into a quarrel with a fellow scout, Albert Mylott. The two boys began fighting and Hall struck Mylott behind the ear with a large clasp knife. The wound inflicted required stitching. Hall immediately pleaded guilty to the charge and, after being admonished by the magistrate's clerk as to the stupidity of his actions, he was sentenced to be bound over to be of good behaviour for six months.

In Leicester there was some comment on how several recent recruiting parades had not been attended by any boy scouts. The *Leicester Daily Post* of 2 April featured a reply. It stated that since the beginning of the war the scouts had been busy and went on to list some of their accomplishments. These included providing guards at vulnerable points, working as orderlies, assisting at recruitment offices, carting beds, furniture and other items to hospitals and other sites, fitting up houses for Belgian refugees, providing bands to play for departing soldiers, delivering letters, distributing books, magazines and papers for soldiers and sailors, and attending over 100 recruitment meetings. Parading, the article stated, was not a scout's style. The writer commented that if you wanted a job doing it had become widely accepted that you send for a boy scout,

> but advertising himself by parading round the town is not in his line, and while there are others who need to do it to prove their existence, they can continue in their own way, and the Scouts will go on their own, helpful, willing, and cheery in all their work.

The barbed reference to other organisations seems to have been a clear dig at the Boy's Brigade.

Yet another wargame involving the boy scouts took place in April involving troops from the South Wigstons and Narborough. The game involved the South Wigstons being responsible for getting a small convoy through the village of Blaby which was defended by the boys of the Narborough Troop. This was, yet again, a clear indication that, despite protests to the contrary, the scouting movement was indeed becoming increasingly militarised by the war.

The beginning of May saw the press cover a somewhat remarkable, perhaps unbelievable, account of a boy scout being attacked by suspected spies. Mr Joy, the scoutmaster at Sheringham in Norfolk, related how he and his troop had been drilling on a hillside when some of the boys reported seeing flashes which looked like signals. A little later it was noticed that one of the scouts, the scoutmaster's son in fact, was missing. Mr Joy eventually discovered his son, unconscious beneath a hedge and with his scout handkerchief bound around his mouth. Upon regaining consciousness, the boy related how he had distinctly seen two men, one of whom looked foreign and was carrying a revolver, signalling with a lamp. When the two men realised they had been observed, they had thrown the lad to the ground and bound the handkerchief around his mouth. The victim was examined by a doctor who stated 'that something undoubtedly happened to the boy to cause hysteria'.[9]

May also saw a Dunfermline boy scout seriously injured in an accident. Robert Munro (10) had been gathering firewood with other boy scouts in a quarry at Dunduff when a sheep at the top of the quarry dislodged a stone which fell, striking Munro on the head. Munro was quickly taken to the Dunfermline and West Fife Hospital where a fractured skull was diagnosed and an immediate operation undertaken. The operation was a success and Munro recovered.

Although the Scouts Defence Corps had found widespread favour, such enthusiasm did not result in large numbers coming forward everywhere. On 20 January the Exeter Association of Boy Scouts set itself an ambitious target. A platoon of thirty-two members had already been successfully formed but it had been decided that a target of establishing a full company of 128 members (a further three platoons) by 10 February be set. The association realised that this was an ambitious target given the time frame, but was hopeful as it believed that the corps so far had been given little publicity locally and that a press campaign would aid in this respect. It was hoped that the establishment of a full company might entice the Chief Scout himself to Exeter to present the boys who had passed through their training with the red feathers which was part of the uniform of the defence corps. The eventual hope was that a full battalion of four companies could be raised.

One of the problems of enticing boys to join the defence corps was the extra equipment which was required and which the scout was expected to supply himself. This included an extra blanket, an extra pair of stout boots, a waterproof sheet, an extra flannel shirt, extra socks or stockings, and a greatcoat. Each patrol was issued with its own tent and a means of carrying it, either on a bicycle carrier or a trek-cart, and, until arms could be supplied, scouts' staves were carried for manual and bayonet training.

Having already seen how valuable the service of scouts and sea scouts was in helping to guard the coast of Britain it was no surprise that the press continued to cover this aspect of the association. Many of the actual patrol duties had, by this stage of the war, been taken over either by Territorial battalions who were waiting for their posting to the front or by the various cyclist battalions. The scouts, however, continued to aid these efforts. The London Cyclists, for example, were helped by the employment of sea scouts who kept watch from elevated locations and could signal the cyclists if anything untoward was detected. The fact that many of the scouts were trained signallers proved of great benefit to the system.

A visit by the founder of the Boy Scouts was always reason for a parade, and when Sir Robert Baden-Powell and his wife visited Knockdolian House in Colmonell in July 1915, some forty-six of the South Ayrshire Boy Scouts paraded. Sir Robert inspected them in great detail and was treated to a display of signalling before he gave a short and encouraging speech to the boys. In this he told them that they were at the forefront of the campaign to replace the men who had gone off to serve their King. The Boy Scouts, he told them, currently had 1,800 members undertaking coastguard duty for the Admiralty while a great many others were undertaking orderly work in hospitals or government offices. Sir Robert concluded by telling the boys to remember always to honour God and their King, to obey the Scout law and to do a good turn daily.

The sheer number of Boy Scouts who joined up to serve in the forces continues to amaze. By the summer the movement in Sussex claimed that 200 officers from the local scouts' association and over

Sea Scouts
at watch
atop a tower.
(The Sphere)

1,000 former scouts were with the forces, with eighteen of them having already been killed in action, eight wounded and four taken prisoner. The local movement was rightfully proud of this contribution to the war effort and throughout the war scouts who were of age were exhorted to enlist.

By the time the bulk of recruits for Kitchener's New Army had been processed, many of the more than 10,000 former scouts and scout officers who had joined up in the first months of the war were experienced officers or NCOs and, with the New Army battalions almost universally lacking experienced leadership, these former scouts provided a sturdy backbone to many of the New Army units.

Many of the New Army battalions made eager use not just of the former scouts mentioned above who had been posted in, but also of the high numbers of scouts who themselves volunteered for service in the New Army units which were being formed across the country. For example, 5 Highland Light Infantry (HLI) had a company of 240 men who were all former scouts, while it also had a detached section of scouts who ran an advanced dressing station.

The fact that the boy scouts were a uniformed presence could sometimes make them a target for those who bore a resentment against the authorities. At the end of June a court in Burnley heard the case of a Patrick Coleman (50) who had been drunk and had interrupted a Salvation Army service by shouting and swearing and then afterwards had come across a young boy scout in the street. He had hit the little lad in the face and knocked him down. Coleman was found guilty and fined the sum of 15s or face imprisonment for thirteen days.

Not all boy scouts, however, were the epitome of the Scout Law. Some boys fell prey to avarice and disgraced the association. Towards the end of June a boy scout from Vauxhall found himself sentenced to receive six strokes of the birch after being convicted of theft. Frederick Roenall had been going around the local hospitals telling wounded soldiers that he had been sent by his scoutmaster to see if there was anything that he could do for them. The wounded men sent him on errands for which they paid him but he simply appropriated the money.

Over the summer the boy scouts enjoyed their annual summer camps. The summer camp was one of the most anticipated events for every troop and attendance was always high. For those troops from urban areas the camps gave the boys the chance to practise many of the skills they had been taught in rural conditions for the very first time and were a valuable learning experience.

The first day of July also saw the Chipping Norton and District Association hold its annual rally. The highlight of this were the various competitions which were held. Troops involved were from Great Rollright, Kingham Hill, Chipping Norton, Salford and Chadlington. A large number of spectators attended and the voluntary collection for wartime charities proved a success. The competitions consisted of: rope bridge building; relay tree-felling race (using posts instead of trees); cooking; signalling, tent pitching and striking; ambulance; and a relay race. At stake was a challenge shield for the troop to win the most points. The shield went to the Peacocks of the Pioneer (Chipping Norton) Troop who won the rope bridge, tree-felling, and signalling competitions while finishing second on the cooking competition.

Although the boy scouts had found favour with the authorities they were often viewed with ridicule or even hostility by other boys, especially in urban areas. The meeting of the Manchester Assizes in July saw the aftermath of an incident where this mutual hostility had gotten out of control with a tragic outcome. The defendant was Harold Brown (16), a troop leader with the Preston Troop. The jury returned a verdict of 'no true bill' on the charges but the prosecution went on to prosecute for a charge of manslaughter under a coroner's warrant. The prosecution outlined the case, saying that on the evening in question Harold and eight or nine of his troop had been practising, with official permission, signalling in the grounds of an unoccupied residence. The garden had a number of fruit trees and a group of boys from the town had been attracted by the trees and invaded the premises. The scouts warned the other boys off but they returned; after being chased away by the scouts they once again returned, this time with reinforcements, and stones were thrown by the town boys with one striking Harold. A scout suggested that a very old miniature rifle that the troop used for target practice should be brought out and four warning shots were fired. The defence made clear that the shots had been fired into the ground and were not aimed at anyone, but the third shot ricocheted and struck one of the town boys in the thigh. The boy, Thomas Mathers (14), suffered a severed artery and bled to death. Mathers' father was currently a prisoner of war in Germany.

When the police had arrived on the scene, they found the accused bleeding from where he had been struck by a stone. When questioned he had stated: 'I got a rifle and fired a shot at them, and they say I hit one of them.'[10] Several of the troop gave evidence that the shots had indeed been fired into the ground and a doctor testified that the bullet wound had, in his opinion, been caused by a ricochet. At this point the jury stepped in and said that they did not wish to hear any more evidence and wished to return a verdict of not guilty. The judge seemingly agreed as, when he was discharging the defendant, he stated that he believed that the case had been the result of a pure accident and that the defendant had no intention of doing any harm.

At Wolverhampton a tragic incident resulted in the award of the Royal Humane Society's bronze medal for bravery to a 9-year-old scout. On 18 July Samuel Ward had been playing with his two sisters when the two girls fell into a deep water-filled pit. Samuel jumped in to rescue them without hesitation but was only able to save his youngest sister while the eldest drowned. Samuel was the son of a soldier and the grandson of a former Wolverhampton Wanderers footballer.

The scout movement was not a success everywhere, however. In August a meeting was held at Leominster with the aim of reinvigorating the movement locally. The meeting was presided over by Major General Sir Elliott Wood, the county commissioner for Herefordshire. Sir Elliott opened his address by telling of his sorrow at how the Leominster Troop, which had began with great enthusiasm, had gradually dwindled and eventually sank so low that there was barely a scout in the town. After holding up the 1st Westminster Troop as an example, Sir Elliott commented that a great many scouts and scoutmasters had joined the colours and that 'was the sort of thing they wanted here in Leominster'. Describing the aims of the recruitment drive he added that what was not needed was a great many boys who thought it might be fun to be a scout, but rather a smaller number who were truly dedicated and knew that being a scout, while fun, was also business. Certainly, he added, scouts had a great deal of fun, especially when on camps, but the main focus of scouting was to build and improve character. The new recruits must have a strong sense of honour and know that by becoming a scout they had become members of 'a magnificent body of boys and young men who were carrying out the obligation' of the movement throughout the country. Sir Elliott then explained why he felt the Leominster scouting movement had failed the first time around. He blamed this on the first troop having gone too fast after its initial creation. Badges, he felt, were awarded too easily and, as result, the boys lost interest. This time around he hoped that badges would have to be truly earned.

The Reverend F.C. Thomas then addressed the assembly, telling them that he believed that the one thing that was most needed was some enthusiasm. The Reverend had brought over the Knighton Troop to serve as an example of what could be achieved. Keenness would be all-important to the re-establishment of the local troop. The Reverend then emphasised that the scouts had three key requirements. Firstly, that of honour and loyalty to King and country. Secondly, absolute obedience to the scoutmasters. Thirdly, to carry out the duty of kindness to others.

The Mayor then explained his belief that the first attempt at establishing the movement, which had taken place in 1910, had failed largely due to the fact that scoutmasters and assistant scoutmasters seemed to have been regularly promoted and sent elsewhere in the district and that there had been a great deal of difficulty in replacing these men. The Leominster Troop had begun with around fifty boys but this number had dwindled while recruitment had not kept pace and by the time of the current meeting there were just fifteen members under an assistant scoutmaster. The Mayor went on to say that he and several other gentlemen of the town felt it was their duty to help reinvigorate the troop, and for that to succeed a new scoutmaster had to be obtained. This they had done in the form of the headmaster of the local secondary school, Mr Drennan. He was sure that under Mr Drennan's leadership the troop would become a success. Concluding his speech, the Mayor stated that he was sure the people of Leominster would be supportive of their efforts and that the sum of £15 had already been raised for the establishment of a drum and fife band.

In a short speech the new scoutmaster told the assembly that he would be demanding a great deal of sacrifice and dedication from the new recruits and it was his belief that, by training as a scout, boys could become 'the grandest creatures in the world'.[11] He concluded that the boys would face hard work and urged any boy who was not prepared to face this not to join.

One of the prime motivations for local authorities to give extensive support to their local scouting associations was that with many council workers having enlisted there was a dearth of labour available for many tasks and the scouts could often help to plug this gap. In some areas, for example, the scouts took over the role of the many lamplighters who had gone to war and it became a common sight to see a scout, mounted on his bicycle, going around the town lighting the gas lamps.

August also saw the death of a boy scout from Sutton Mill, Keighley, in tragic and somewhat mysterious circumstances. Clarence Whiteoak (13) had attended a meeting of his troop and returned home before retiring to bed at around 9.30 pm. His brother Fred went to bed half an hour later (without a light) and when he got into bed he felt his brother's feet near to the pillow. Assuming that his brother was playing a prank he went to sleep. Shortly after he awoke when his mother went upstairs and

Sea Scout lights a lamp at Mortlake where they had taken over the duty.
(Illustrated Sporting and Dramatic News)

discovered Clarence was dead, suspended by a cord from the top of the iron bedstead. At the subsequent inquest Clarence's father stated that, as far as he knew, the lad did not have a care in the world. He knew that he had been practising knot tying and feared that his son had been experimenting with knots when he accidentally met his death. The jury returned a verdict that they did not have sufficient evidence to establish how the strangulation had been brought about.

Another boy scout met his death in August. James McLean had led an unfortunate and tough life, being previously an inmate of the Rossie Reformatory for two years, but he had joined the boy scouts in an effort to make something of himself. He was a native of Rosehearty, Fraserburgh, and 10 August found 16-year-old James serving coastguard duty at a station at Montrose. On the day in question two 18-year-old privates from the 2/1 Highland Cyclist Corps were on duty with James at the Links. The soldiers had placed their rifles in a hut and James had picked one up. The other soldier also picked up his loaded rifle but it was discharged accidentally and James was hit in the jaw and neck, dying instantly.

Motherwell hosted a large gathering of scouts in late August when a Boy Scouts' rally was held in the town. The rally involved approximately 400 scouts from Motherwell, Wishaw, Bellshill, Mossend, Larkhall, Stonehouse, Dalserf, Coatbridge and Strathaven. The scouts assembled at Knowetop under the command of Sergeant Barbour and Corporal Emmet of 12 Cameronians (Scottish Rifles) and were led into the town by the town band. Arriving on the inspection field the scouts paraded and were inspected by Colonel R. King-Stewart of Murdostoun Castle and other dignitaries. After the march-past, which the colonel commented was exceptionally well performed, the colonel addressed the boys. During this address he told the boys that, in his opinion, the Boy Scouts Association was doing work every bit as valuable as a munitions' worker or soldier. After refreshments had been taken the boys gave several displays over the course of the afternoon. Many of these demonstrations had a military overtone. They included bayonet drill by 1st Bellshill Troop, muster at arms by 2nd Motherwell Troop, bridge-building by 3rd and 4th Motherwell Troops, and a novel display of life-saving using rocket apparatus by 4th Motherwell Troop. Sadly, the weather turned poor and many of the spectators had left by the time the later demonstrations took place while several, including signalling, ambulance work, and field telegraphy had to be cancelled. At the end of the rally the scoutmaster of the 4th Motherwell Troop was awarded the fleur-de-lys for the most original and clever display. The rally ended with the singing of the National Anthem.

One of the aims of the scouts was to gather into its ranks those 'bad boys' in order to turn the energies of such miscreants towards more correct channels in which he might become of use to society and to ensure that he developed personally into a healthy and honourable man. In Aberdeen, the local scoutmasters gathered together to explore this issue more thoroughly and every officer was encouraged to prepare suggestions for subsequent meetings. Aberdonian scouts were also strongly encouraged throughout the year to qualify for the fireman and handyman proficiency badges, while those who already possessed the ambulance and missioner badges to keep up their skills in these proficiencies as they might prove extremely useful in the event of an emergency.

Even as late as September some scouts were still maintaining guard over some locations in parts of Scotland. In Aberdeenshire the detachments on guard at Bridge of Don and Belhelvie were inspected by commissioner Giffen. The commissioner inspected the boys and was extremely pleased by what he found. Particular praise was reserved for the detachment at Belhelvie who, making the most of the weather conditions, were still camping under canvas. This detachment had been under the command of patrol leader G. Hay of the 23rd Aberdeen Troop for some time and he was praised for the way in which he maintained morale and kept work going. Now that the holiday season was over and boys were returning to school, however, concerns were raised that there might not be enough scouts available to maintain these guards.

As a result, an appeal was sent out for any scouts who could undertake the duties to contact Scoutmaster Norrie who would make arrangements.

On 28 October the Gateshead and District Boy Scouts Association held its seventh annual meeting. The annual report of the association stated that, although a detailed census was made impossible due to the fact that so many officers had joined the forces, the reports that had been obtained were positive and hinted that the association was strengthening. The association consisted of thirty-two registered troops which was an increase of ten from the previous year and an increase of nineteen from 1913. There were approximately 1,300 officers and scouts which was an increase of 500 from the previous year and 950 from 1913. An increase in the number of proficiency badges could also be reported, with 786 badges being awarded compared to 511 in 1914. The report also commented on the former members now with the forces. It listed sixteen scoutmasters, twenty-eight assistant scoutmasters, nine instructors, twenty-six patrol leaders, eleven scouts and three troop committee members. This amounted to ninety-three members of the association and thus far twenty-four troops had suffered the loss of a member or former member in action at the front. The district scoutmaster and assistant county commissioner, Mr H. Gillies Wicks, submitted his own report in which he stated that in his seven-and-a-half years with the association he had never known a year when greater advances had been made, and also commented on the fact that the Gateshead association had provided a permanent coastguard patrol at three points on the Northumberland coast. The reports were adopted on the motion of the Reverend H.S. Stephenson (rector of Gateshead) who commented on the 'splendid way in which the Scouts Association had risen to the occasion during the war', and said the Boy Scout movement was responsible for 'a great improvement in the national character'.[12]

Baden-Powell had been deeply affected by the necessity of the few recreation huts run by the YMCA in France. By November he was actively engaged in raising funds through the Boy Scouts Association. The scouts worked in close association with the YMCA to raise funds for additional huts. On 5 November he wrote to General Allenby to gauge the requirements for recreation huts and eleven days later he had just returned from a tour of Liverpool and Manchester during which he had been promised the sum of approximately £12,000 for the cause. By the middle of December the first hut to be funded by the scouts was erected at Etaples.

Military Service

The year 1915 opened with the news of the death of a former scout from London. Private Lewin E. Moat had formerly been a patrol leader and then an instructor with the 2nd West London (St Cuthbert's) Troop but had joined the ranks of 13 London (The Kensington's) Regiment. Aged just 19, he was killed in action on 9 January and is buried at Rue-De-Bacquerot (13th London) Graveyard.

With a great many soldiers training in Britain it was inevitable that there would be fatal accidents. On 18 January Corporal Eldrick Webb Garrod of 1st Suffolk Battery, East Anglian Brigade, Royal Field Artillery, was one of several mounted men dispatched to scout out the area around Cavenham, Suffolk. Corporal Garrod (20) was an experienced man in the battery, having served in it for four years. Before the war he had been a printer and a troop leader with the 3rd Lowestoft Troop of boy scouts. At around 11 am Garrod's commanding officer, Captain Kenyon, was notified that the corporal's horse had returned by itself and a search was quickly organised. A body was found shortly afterwards and identified as being that of Corporal Garrod. A subsequent coroner's inquest, which resulted in a verdict of accidental death, revealed that Corporal Garrod's horse had probably stumbled in a rabbit hole and he had suffered a fractured skull when he was thrown. Captain Kenyon stated at the inquest that Corporal Garrod had been much respected by both officers and men in the battery and that his death seemed as worthy as dying at the front. He also expressed his sympathy to Corporal Garrod's mother, who had six sons serving.[13]

On 31 January another young former scout was killed in action. Private William Ireland was aged just 18 when he joined up in Kitchener's Army. Clearly, he had been judged a good and competent soldier as he had been transferred to 1 Worcesters and sent to France in mid-January. Unfortunately, the former scout was not long at the front before he was killed in action and his parents in Cropthorne, near Evesham, were notified of his death in February.[14]

Charles Dutton was a member of the 1st Doe Lea Troop and was like many scouts at the outbreak of war. Brought up as a firm Christian and imbued with the dedication to loyalty and duty common to the scouts of the time, he had been determined to do his bit and had joined up, aged 19 on 2 September 1914. He had joined the 2 Lincolnshire and been posted to Grimsby for six months. In February 1915 he was posted to France. Private Dutton, who had previously been employed at Glapwell Colliery, was at the front for just eight weeks when he was shot in the neck and killed on 19 April.[15]

1915 continued to take a heavy toll of those who had joined up at the start of the war. Charles Henry Raymond West was the son of the secretary of the Boy Scouts Association in County Louth and had himself been involved with the movement. At the outbreak of war he

had secured a commission as a 2nd Lieutenant in 6 Middlesex Regiment and while training with his battalion had distinguished himself as an exceptional marksman. On 1 April 1915 he was promoted to the rank of lieutenant and posted to the 4th Battalion of the Middlesex Regiment in France. Unfortunately, Lieutenant West (21) was only at the front for around two months before he was killed in action.[16]

As we have already seen, the scouting movement had spread far and wide across the colonies of the British Empire. On 18 June yet another of these 'colonial' scouts lost his life in

Private Charles Dutton.
(Derbyshire Courier)

service to King and country. Lance Corporal Hugh Alan Thompson of 1 Border Regiment was aged just 18 when he was killed at Gallipoli. He was the son of Joseph and Angela Thompson of Rangoon, Burma, where he had been a scout.[17]

The training which was given to Boy Scouts made for a good background for service in the army and many went on to obtain commissions. In July it was announced that Private Ronald Orme Crookes from Burton had

Lieutenant C.H.R. West. (Illustrated Sporting and Dramatic News)

been commissioned as a 2nd Lieutenant in 24 Royal Fusiliers (the so-called Sportsman's Battalion). Crookes had been patrol leader at Branstone and in 1913 had won third prize in the fencing competition at the great Scout Exhibition in Birmingham. He had enlisted in October 1914 but his capabilities had been quickly recognised and he had thus been marked for a commission.

Many former scouts wrote home to tell of their experiences at the front. Many of these accounts found their way into the press and were used to buoy the morale not only of the general populace, but also to demonstrate to current scouts just how proud they should be of the organisation. In September one such account was published in the *Bedfordshire Times and Independent*. The account was written by Signaller A. Carr to his brother at Stratton Street, Biggleswade. It described how Signaller Carr, serving with 1/5 Bedfordshire at Gallipoli, had taken part in fierce fighting during a recent attack. The 19-year-old former scout told his brother how proud he would have been of the regiment when it made an attack, supported by two London Territorial battalions, on a heavily defended Turkish hillside position. Despite losing many officers and men, the 'Beds' had succeeded in taking the hill within two hours; they had been forced to fight 'like demons' and had subsequently been given the nickname 'The Yellow Devils'. In a more sombre tone Signaller Carr continued to explain how his officer and three or four of his fellow signallers, including a close friend of his, were wounded and one killed; those who had come through unscathed could not believe it. He also complained over not receiving mail from home, despite the fact that he had written several times. Signaller Carr survived the Gallipoli campaign but, like many others who had fought in this campaign, the now Lance Sergeant Carr found himself fighting in Palestine. Sadly, he was killed during the Third Battle of Gaza on 3 November 1917.

The fighting at Gallipoli was ferocious and casualties among former scouts were high. Among them was a former scout from Berwick. Private John Hendry had been a Territorial with 1/4 King's Own Scottish Borderers and the son of a local priest, the Rev. P.G. Hendry of Paxton Manse. Prior to the war he had been studying law but he was killed, aged just 20, on 12 July.[18]

As the fighting at Gallipoli continued, yet another notable scout lost his life. Corporal Samuel Sumption of 'C' Squadron, Dorset (Queen's Own) Yeomanry was killed on 27 August, aged 28. Originally from Wimborne in Dorset, Corporal Sumption had been scoutmaster of 1 Wimborne Troop. After moving to Egypt he had organised the first troop of scouts in that country and had received a commendation from Sir Robert Baden-Powell for this feat. A married man, Corporal Sumption left behind his American widow, Mabel Alice Keeler Sumption of Brooklyn, New York.[19]

The Battle of Loos was the main allied offensive of 1915. The battle saw the first use of gas by the British and the battlefield debut of New Army units. Despite this the offensive was an overall failure with only limited gains and very heavy casualties sustained. The offensive lasted from 25 September to 8 October and by the end the British had suffered over 59,000 casualties. Among the units thrown into the attack on the first day was 2/8 Gurkha Rifles. The day was disastrous for the Gurkhas but demonstrated their unparalleled courage. The Gurkhas threw themselves repeatedly against the heavy German defences but suffered appalling losses. By the end of the day the 2/8 Gurkha Rifles had lost 750 men of their 800-strong complement. Only one officer and forty-nine other ranks were left to answer roll-call at the end of the day. Among the officers to be killed on this fateful day was 2nd Lieutenant Ernest Alexander Meldrum (23). Lieutenant Meldrum was in the Indian Army Reserve of Officers and was attached to the Gurkhas. He was a native of Musselburgh, the son of Major Alexander Pearson Meldrum, where he had been the assistant scoutmaster of the 1st Musselburgh Troop. When the district commissioner inspected the troop in the summer of 1916 Major Meldrum informed him that more than forty former members of the troop were currently in the firing line.[20]

Another former scout to lose his life on this first day of the battle was 2nd Lieutenant Bernard Urmston Hare of 14 Middlesex (although at the time of his death he was attached to 1 Middlesex). The 22-year-old subaltern was formerly a member of the Artist Rifles Officer Training Corps and scoutmaster of 66 North London Troop.[21]

The Royal Navy, while the mightiest single navy in the world, was still utilising some ships which were of the pre-dreadnought class and which dated back to the turn of the century. One of these was HMS *Formidable*; on 31 December she had taken part in exercises in the English Channel with the rest of the 5th Battle Group, without any destroyer screen to protect from submarines. The early hours of 1 January found the 5th Battle Group still in the Channel, despite warnings of submarine activity. Shortly after 2 am, HMS *Formidable* was torpedoed by a German U-Boat. Despite the fact that it took almost 2½ hours for her to sink, the rough seas made it difficult to pick up survivors. Only 157 men were rescued while 547 officers and men lost their lives. Among the thirty-five officers to be lost was Surgeon Septimus Hibbert who had previously been a member of the 7th St Pancras Troop.

At least one more former scout was killed in the loss of HMS *Formidable*. Private Arthur John Tungate (19) was formerly a member of 1st Blyth Troop and had worked at the local colliery before joining the Royal Marine Light Infantry. His parents lived at 5 Stone Row, Bebside Furnace, Northumberland. HMS *Formidable* had been moored next to HMS *Bulwark* on 26 November 1914 when the latter ship suffered a disastrous accidental explosion which destroyed her utterly and resulted in the deaths of all but nine of her crew. Private Tungate had written home to his sister describing the incident. In his letter he described how the explosion had left only small pieces of debris from the *Bulwark* and how, within seconds, there had been nothing but smoke, pieces of wood, bodies and body parts on the water. The horrific sight had obviously terrified the young man and he said 'It was a horrible sight, and I trust I may never again in my life see such a scene.'[22] Tragically, the young former scout's life was to last just a further month.[23] At least one former scout had lost his life in the *Bulwark* explosion. Boy 1st Class Cecil James Gasson had formerly been a member of the 1st Oldham Troop at Rotherwick.[24]

As we have seen the loyal and dutiful nature of the scouts resulted in many members joining up as soon as they were able and huge numbers enlisted during the first two years of the war. In Essex the members of the 1st Brentwood Troop (which was divided into two patrols, named hounds and ravens) could boast that all of the eleven members who had been camped at Woodham Walter in 1913 were now serving with the colours. They included scoutmasters Captain Land, Captain Hoare and Corporal Pond (in 1913 the latter was a patrol leader), patrol leader Pockock, and scouts Atkins, Hepworth, Martins, Peters, Riches, Rudd and Westwood. Towards the end of November Corporal Pond was home on leave and described his experiences to his former troop. His reminiscences included an account of his participation in the Battle of Frezenberg Ridge which took place on 13 May 1915 as part of the wider Second Battle of Ypres and had been the first battle in which the Essex Yeomanry had really been involved. The regiment had suffered 161 casualties on the day, including the loss of its commanding officer, Lieutenant Colonel Edmund Deacon. The remainder of his talk focused on the activities of a cavalry regiment which had found itself largely redundant and was therefore utilised as dismounted troops in line-holding duties in the trenches.[25]

For many families the war did not only bring the agony of loss of a loved one but this was often presaged by the additional purgatory of not knowing the fate of a loved one for many months, sometimes years. Such families often went through the agonies of searching for any possible news of their lost loved ones. Private C.W. Marsden of Staveley, Derbyshire, was the former assistant scoutmaster of the Staveley Town Troop and was employed at a munitions factory in Sheffield but felt the need to do more; he left the factory to enlist in January 1915 and was posted to the Northumberland Fusiliers. Such was the desperate need for men that he sailed for France the next month. Private Marsden experienced a hard time of it, being involved in several major battles and losing the forefinger on his left hand when it was shot away. Despite this, he carried on but his family were notified in December that Private Marsden had been posted missing in October, thus began a desperate search for information. His sister, Mrs Dranfield of 89 Silverdales, Dinnington, near Rotherham, placed appeals in the press for anyone with information to get in touch with her.

On 23 October the battered 1/7 Northumberland Fusiliers were manning trenches near Armentieres during a relatively quiet period, but even then front-line trench duty was still dangerous due to shelling, sniping and raiding. On 23 October (the night before the battalion was relieved) Lance Corporal James Evans (20) was killed. James was a native of Berwick and a former scout there. His parents, James and Isabella, perhaps inspired by their bitterness over his death, had a rather curious, inscription placed upon his headstone in Bailleul Communal Cemetery Extension, Nord. It reads 'HIS VIRTUES ARE RECORDED ELSEWHERE'.

Pvt C.W. Marsden.
(Derbyshire Courier)

In many cases there was some confusion over the fate of men who had been reported as casualties. This often led to families suffering extended periods of grief before they were notified that a loved one had been confirmed as a casualty. In some cases, however, there was a happier ending. Private Ernest Booth of the village of Clowne in Derbyshire had been a prominent member of the 1st Clowne Troop of boy scouts and had gone abroad with the Broadsworth St John Ambulance Brigade which was attached to the medical unit of the Royal Naval Division. Private Booth landed with the first wave at the Dardanelles. A few days after the landing his family received the news that he had been killed. Private Booth was in fact alive and the report was amended later. He had experienced a very narrow escape after a German aircraft dropped a bomb near his dugout. Booth was wounded in the head and foot and taken to hospital at Alexandria. He had been in hospital for a fortnight when he contracted enteric fever. By October, Private Booth had written to his family that he had arrived back in England and was being well cared for by the Royal Army Medical Corps and St John's staff at Charing Cross Hospital.

Private Ernest Booth, reported killed but only wounded. (The Derbyshire Courier)

Many former scouts had emigrated to the colonies before the war but, fired by their upbringing in a spirit of loyalty and duty, volunteered for service either by returning to the mother country, or by joining the forces of their adopted countries. Among the latter was George Henry Evans. A native of Berwick-upon-Tweed, George had been a scout there and had subsequently emigrated to Canada. He joined the Canadian Army where he became a Sergeant in 10 Canadian Infantry. He was killed in action on 20 November, aged 25. For his parents this was a terrible blow as they had lost a younger son just a month previously. His parents had the same inscription placed upon his headstone at Maple Leaf Cemetery as appears on that of his brother, who had been killed just weeks earlier.

In Berwick, news broke that Lieutenant Frank Weddell Smail, a former Berwick Scout, had succumbed to his wounds and died on 1 December. Lieutenant Smail was the son of Henry Richardson Smail and had been a Territorial and officer in 'D' Company of 1/7 Northumberland Fusiliers, sent across to France with the rest of his unit and thrown into the slaughter almost immediately. In June they had taken part in an attack and suffered heavy casualties. Between 22 and 28 June the battalion was manning trenches and once again suffered casualties, among them Lieutenant Smail; he had been wounded and brought home for treatment. He is buried in his home town.

On 30 December the liner SS *Persia* was steaming off Crete when she was torpedoed and sunk by U-boat *U-38*. The attack came without warning and was hugely controversial as it broke several established international naval laws regarding the launching of attacks on neutral merchant vessels. These agreements stated that such vessels could be stopped and searched but only sunk if passengers and crew were put in a place of safety first (not including lifeboats on the open sea). Of the 519 people aboard, 343 were killed when the liner sank. Among them was a former Berwick scout who had gone on to become a scoutmaster in India. By 1915 he was a lieutenant in the Indian Army Reserve of Officers, attached to 2/3 Queen Alexandra's Own Gurkha Rifles. On 30 December he was a passenger aboard the SS *Persia* and was one of those who lost his life. Lieutenant Robertson (29) was the son of the Berwick Boy Scouts commissioner.[26]

CHAPTER 3

1916

Home Front

We have already seen how the scouts got involved in a wide variety of wartime charities. The members of the various troops were often at the heart of these fundraising efforts but with their motto of doing good deeds the scouts also ensured that they donated as freely as possible to other charities in which they were not directly involved. The efforts of the scouting movement in providing charitable funds was a way in

Lady Webster selling to Boy Scouts at a fete at Battle Abbey. (The Graphic)

which they could directly support the war effort and fulfil a part of their scouting pledge.

Women had always been accepted as scoutmasters but with many male scoutmasters and other officers of the movement joining up and serving at the front, there was a shortage of suitable male candidates in some places. Many more women, therefore, stepped forward to fill these gaps. Many were women from the upper-classes and some had very varied and unusual skills and experiences which were of use to the movement. In February 1916 one of these women, Miss Phyllis Scrimgeour of Hemsby Hall, Norfolk, was married to a staff surgeon in the Royal Navy. She had led an adventurous life before the war, being noted as a skilled motorist, golfer and skier who had 'once spent a whole winter in Lapland in Lap costume'.[1]

Unsurprisingly, the majority of boy scouts wished to become actively involved in raising funds for the various wartime causes, but there were several issues facing such endeavours. The most serious problem was that the boy scout code forbade scouts to accept money for nothing. They were permitted, and indeed encouraged, to earn as much as they could honestly but never to beg. Thus, the boy scouts did not have the flag days that became a part of so many charities during the war and had to find alternative means of raising funds. The way that the boys found was to collect and resell glass and earthenware bottles and containers. In January, boy scouts in Leicester were active in collecting bottles to be resold with the profits being donated to a variety of wartime charities.

Former scoutmaster, Mrs Phyllis Greig (née Scrimgeour) of Hemsby Hall. (The Graphic)

Leicester Boy Scout collecting bottles with his cart. (Leicester Daily Post)

In February the Boy Scouts in Belfast decided that they were going to gather £600 to allow the purchase, construction and running of a recreation hut for soldiers at the front. Across Belfast people were encouraged to donate old bottles to the scouts and by the end of March some 500,000 bottles had been collected and were being sorted and graded.

Bottle collections quickly became a focal point of many scouting campaigns. In June, for example, the 4th Motherwell Troop was collecting bottles, the proceeds of the sale to be donated to various war relief funds. Residents were encouraged to donate generously while also being warned that they should donate only to uniformed scouts who would be carrying an official warrant allowing them to collect the bottles. In the following month the scouts in Kirkcaldy were collecting bottles and jars to fund more scout huts at the front, while in September, scouts at Faversham sold 1,300 medicine bottles raising £2 14s 1d for the local military hospital.

The bottle campaigns used to provide recreation huts continued throughout the war and were joined by schemes to provide funds for motor ambulances and other vital amenities. Added to the collection of bottles was the collection of waste paper. In Devon, scouts collected huge amounts of paper and used the money raised to fund a side-car with trailer and transporter for the Red Cross.

Above left: *Belfast Boy Scouts bottle collection advert.* (Whig Times)

Above right: *Kirkcaldy Boy Scouts bottle collection advert.* (Fifeshire Advertiser)

The reduction in age limits for the Scouts Defence Corps had proved to be controversial and by 1916 it had been reversed and the corps was, once again, open only to boys aged over 16. Many local corps, however, seem to have happily ignored this instruction if a parental permission form was supplied.

Despite the fact that invasion and even raiding seemed far less likely now and the far greater number of troops available to defend Britain, the Scouts Defence Corps stood some 6,000-strong by mid-February. By now the force was beginning to acquire additional specialties in addition to its infantry training. Units were encouraged to specialise in signalling, bridge-building, dispatch riding, ambulance work, transport, army service duties or ordnance shop work. Thus, the corps was attempting to branch outwards in an effort to maintain its value despite the lessening risk of invasion. The association was also keen to point out that the training itself was of great use to a boy in his future life. Some 20,000 scouts had now served in the forces and the reports which came back about them tended to reinforce the belief that training as a scout prepared a boy for life as a soldier at the front. Sir Robert Baden-Powell argued that drill of a military nature played no role in the scouts. Rather it was the contrary, as the scout movement sought to encourage initiative. This was duplicitous in the extreme. While the scouts did not drill as such, the members of the defence corps certainly did and, while initiative was encouraged, so too was total obedience to superiors. The scouts, argued Baden-Powell, had allowed the authorities (whether military or civilian) to recognise that 'the secret of making successful soldiers lies, not as was formerly supposed in giving the lads a thorough instruction in drill and musketry, but in developing, as a first step, a solid foundation of moral character on which to build the future soldier or citizen, whichever is needed.)[2]

The scouts had a tradition of taking part in annual sports days and these continued throughout the war. Often, they were held alongside sports days held by locally based military units and so the boys were made to feel like they were already a part of the great military enterprise. In early March a day of service athletics was held at Blackheath and the day included a series of events for the scouts too. The winners of the 1,000 yards was a team from 5th (Greenwich) Troop and the boys found themselves featured in the *Illustrated Sport and Dramatic News*. It was through such events that the members of the boy scouts were exposed to men who were actually in the military and were inculcated with a sense of duty while the need for physical fitness was encouraged.

The eagerness of the scouts to play their role in the military campaign was praiseworthy, but the military impetus of the movement could sometimes lead to disaster or tragedy. The constant urging for boys to learn how to handle firearms, for example, was sometimes a practice which could end tragically if not properly supervised. In April, a group of Middlesbrough scouts decided to practise their skills with the revolver by shooting at a tin placed in the fork of a tree. One of the boys' revolvers discharged accidentally and another of the scouts, John Francis Coates (16), fell down. The other boys at first thought he was shamming but it was then discovered that a bullet was lodged in his head and he was rushed to hospital where he later died.

In May tragedy struck a group of scouts from Croydon while they were on their annual camp. The boys were encamped at Chalden,

Winners of the 1,000 yards race. (Illustrated Sporting and Dramatic News)

near Caterham, and a group of them were sitting in the shade of a large elm tree when a large branch fell onto them. One of the boys, Norman Charles Cowling (11), was badly injured and died on his way to hospital.

Among the many duties which the scouts undertook in wartime was the staffing of the numerous canteens which sprung up across Britain. Many of these were based in railway stations, while others were based in various buildings in towns and cities across the country. All provided much needed comfort to the soldiers, sailors and airmen who found themselves having to make their way across the land on leave or for a posting. One of the largest canteens was the Buffet canteen at Victoria Station. The staff of the canteen were primarily female volunteers aided by the Boy Scouts, and word of the Buffet's policy of not charging for their food and drink quickly spread, making it immensely popular with soldiers arriving off the many leave-trains. Many a London-based Boy Scout spent his day serving men who had come fresh from the trenches or men who were about to depart for the front. Once again, this was one of the largely unremarked but nevertheless incredibly useful duties which were performed by the scouts throughout the war.

Empire Day brought news of awards to two prominent members of the Hull Association. Mr Herbert Dunkerley was the county commissioner for sea scouts in both Yorkshire and Northumberland and his task since the war began had been an extremely arduous one, overseeing the coastguard duties of such a lengthy and sparsely populated coast. The Chief Scout conferred the high order of the silver wolf upon Mr Dunkerley. Scoutmaster A.T.S. Wilkinson was scoutmaster of the 1st Hull Troop and had been responsible for organising the local Scouts Defence Corps. The corps had seen some 122 Hull scouts become members and for these services Mr Wilkinson had been awarded the Silver Swastika Thanks Badge.[3]

Despite the wartime demands made of the scouts there was still time for both fun and traditional duties and activities. In early June, the Hull Cyclist Boy Scouts were treated to a magic show. Two days later the boys were on their bicycles on a ride to Warne. A splendid turnout was reported, and the scouts mapped the route carefully for future ventures. Their scoutmaster was also planning a billeting holiday which was to take place for three days over Whitsuntide at Welton Dale in the East Riding of Yorkshire.

Also in June, Admiral Beatty wrote, via the Chief Scout, to the Sea Scouts in Scarborough, which would be forever linked with the horrific German naval raid of 1914 which forged a strong bond between the Royal Navy and the town. The admiral praised the training which boys received in the Sea Scouts and intimated that there were many former Sea Scouts in the ranks of the Royal Navy. All, he believed, had benefited from the training they had received in the scouts. He went on to relate how the captain of HMS *Inconstant* had recently organised a meeting of 200 former scouts and it was hoped that such meetings would take place regularly. They maintained the esprit de corps of the scouting movement and encouraged the sailors who were not a part of that movement.

Walsall Scouts held a camp at St Ronans, Birmingham. There were twelve troops present for the weekend, the 1st, 2nd, 3rd, 5th, 6th , 8th, and 9th Walsall Troops were joined by the Chase Terrace, Darlaston, Troop and visiting troops from Wednesbury, Bishop Latimer, Birmingham and Willenhall. Under the leadership of the district scoutmaster, Commandant Fred Beard, the scouts arrived on the Saturday afternoon and were treated to displays of bridge building, flag signalling and ambulance work by the visiting troops. On the Saturday evening the scouts paraded through the town before being given free time. The Sunday began with a service which was followed by preparations for the forthcoming inspection. While the service was in progress and the 250 or so scouts were absent, the tents and field were inspected by Sir Edward and Lady Holden. Following the service the scouts marched to the cricket ground on Gorway Road where they formed up for inspections by the Mayor, Sir Edward and Lady Holden and others (including military officers and local officers from the scouts). The general salute was followed by the inspection of individual troops and a march past. The Mayor then addressed the scouts, telling them that he was delighted to have been given the opportunity to see them and that the work they were doing was extremely valuable. He assured them that the training they were receiving in the scouts would be of great benefit when they were men and joined the forces. Sunday concluded with another, short, service and the boys retired to bed. The camp was struck the following morning and the scouts went their separate ways. While the event went off very well, Mr Beard appealed in the press for gentlemen or ladies to come forward to be officers in the Walsall scouts.

On 3 July, the Birmingham Boy Scouts assembled for their annual sports day. The event was also marked by a general parade and a parade through the city to the sports field at Cannon Hill Park. Over 5,000 scouts were assembled for this event and a great deal of positive publicity resulted from it. The more traditional sports were also joined by activities and competitions in events such as bridge-building using wooden staves.

Birmingham Boy Scouts bridge-building during the annual sports. (Birmingham Gazette)

Given the good work which scouts had already performed in agriculture, it was no surprise that the government sought to formalise arrangements. In the approach to harvest time in the summer the Ministry of National Service asked specifically for scout labour as the scouts had already proven to be disciplined and reliable. In many areas special camps were set up to house the scouts who were working on the land. To counter claims that the boys' schoolwork would suffer, these camps were overseen by the local authorities which supplied teachers and schemes of education for the boys so that they would not fall behind. In East London, for example, 100 boys over school age but below military age volunteered to go to Peterborough to help weed the flax crop, while a much larger contingent volunteered later in the year to help harvest the flax. The war had resulted in flax becoming a vital wartime crop and, in the Peterborough area alone, some 300 scouts, drawn from eighty East London troops, occupied nine camps. The scouts who undertook agricultural duties under the auspices of the Ministry of National Service were paid 14s for food and an extra 11d per day pay. The weeding and harvesting scouts worked for six hours a day, and so enthusiastic were they that local farmers told the press that the scouts did more work in six hours than the local boys did in ten.

This announcement found the Newcastle Association in some upheaval. The former district commissioner, Mr T.R. Dargue, had recently retired owing to both ill-health and other claims upon his time. Mr F.F. Corballis had been appointed to take over and he was introduced at a meeting held at Spittal Tongues at the beginning of July.

Mr Corballis praised his predecessor, but a large part of his speech concerned the recent appeal for agricultural help. He explained how an agreement had been reached between the Boy Scouts Association, the Farmers' Club and the Dairy Farmers' Association. This agreement put in place nine points.

1. Patrols of six scouts were to be billeted on each farm under responsible leadership.
2. Railway fares and transit costs were to be met by the farmer.
3. Hours of labour were to be limited to a maximum of seven hours per day with regular breaks and no work before breakfast.
4. The boys were to be given three substantial meals per day.
5. Scouts were to provide their own blankets and sleeping kit.
6. Where it was possible, patrols from the same troop were to be billeted on adjoining farms.
7. Daily reports were to be sent in by each patrol, detailing the work done.
8. Farmers should provide suitable sleeping accommodation in barns, granaries or other buildings.
9. That the Boy Scouts Association place the services of the boys at the disposal of the Agricultural War Committee on the understanding that every provision will be made for their welfare.

Mr Corballis also asked for the cooperation of all officers in assisting him in strengthening the movement in Newcastle. 'He was desirous of having the movement placed on a firm basis', and he could see 'no reason why the numbers should not be doubled'. The Newcastle association seems to have been suffering from a lack of organisation and enthusiasm. Mr Corballis further strengthened this impression in his speech when he stated that he hoped that, in the near future, 'every troop in Newcastle-upon-Tyne would have its own headquarters'.[4]

The Newcastle Association found an unusual activity for its scouts to undertake in August. The annual camp, which took place at Keld, in Swaledale in the North Riding of Yorkshire, was unusual in that it took place on a grouse moor during the shooting season. The absence of the customary beaters was filled, innovatively, by the scouts themselves. For the 103 boys present it offered the opportunity for a series of healthy days out on the hills and the boys seemed to have enjoyed the experience. They marched twelve miles from the nearest railway halt with an altitude increase on their march of almost 2,000ft. Despite this arduous march, only four boys had dropped out. The march was led by the drums and bugles of the Scouts and one scout, Drummer Eyre of Heaton Troop, distinguished himself by playing his drum to keep the beat the whole distance. The camp that the boys set up overlooked Swaledale and was highly picturesque and the camp commander was initially Major E. Cyril Burnup, Royal Engineers, who was home on sick leave. Unfortunately, Major Burnup was recalled early to France and had to leave the boys.

A guard was mounted each night and on two occasions 'raids' led by Colonel the Hon. Alfred Sidney and Colonel Thornton were thwarted with the raiders being captured. The hilly terrain of the area enabled the Tyneside boys to substantially improve their scouting skills while the mountain air had a beneficial effect on their general health and appetites.

When the boys were gathered to beat for the guns they formed into three sections, each composed of twenty-five scouts with signallers on the flanks, on a daily basis on two drives. The guns gave high praise to the boys for the efficient way they set about their duties and one effort was deserving of special mention. A drive which had averaged just thirty brace of grouse produced 99½ brace when the scouts were beating. In recognition of the work of the scouts, the guns forwarded the sum of £15 to commissioner Corballis for the provision of prizes for sports, a high tea and a visit to a picture hall when they returned home to Newcastle.

The camp had been an outstanding success and the boys themselves came home in an improved and robust condition having enjoyed themselves greatly after the ten-day long camp.

One of the most successful of the many fundraising efforts on behalf of the Red Cross were the flag days. These efforts were supported by many groups, including the Boy Scouts. The Boy Scouts did not usually sell flags but they did help out by delivering items bought at charity sales. Many Boy Scouts also gathered to organise a delivery service for the delivery of shopping to those who could not get out of the house to collect it themselves.

As we have already seen, the growth of the Scouts Defence Corps was somewhat patchy with some areas being extremely enthusiastic while others were either opposed or ambivalent in their attitudes towards the corps. In Sunderland it would appear that the force had been met with some levels of indifference. As late as the end of August the local association

Boy Scout delivery boy gets directions from Mrs McKenna (the wife of the Chancellor of the Exchequer) in nurses' uniform. (The Sketch)

was appealing for boys aged 16 or over to come forward to 'get the Scouts Defence Corps in full working order'. The boys were encouraged with the promise of the 'the fine opportunity for youths to receive training and drilling of a more or less military character'.[5]

One of the challenges facing the Royal Navy was in finding sufficient shipping space for ferrying wounded servicemen back to Britain. As a result, many liners and other vessels were pressed into service as hospital ships. The largest of these was the RMS *Britannic* of the White Star Line. The sister ship of the RMS *Olympic* and the ill-fated RMS *Titanic*, the *Britannic* was completed in December 1915 and almost immediately commandeered. During 1915–16 the ship was used to ferry wounded troops back to Britain from the Dardanelles. On the morning of 21 November the liner, now the HMHS *Britannic*, was off the Greek island of Kea when she struck a mine. The damage to the *Britannic* proved fatal but the ship took over an hour to sink and of the 1,065 people aboard there were only thirty casualties. Among the crew of the *Britannic* were ten boy scouts. By early December the boys had returned to Britain, landing at Birkenhead on 5 December. During the crisis the boys acquitted themselves superbly and with great bravery. The officers and nurses from the vessel commented on the boys' reactions and their lack of fear. After the ship struck the mine the scouts immediately took up their assigned positions, manning lifts which successfully brought many of the wounded up from below decks. When it became too dangerous for the boys to remain, they had to be ordered to abandon ship and the ten brave scouts slid down 50ft of rope to the waiting lifeboats.

In undertaking coast-watching duties, many boy scouts were being self-sacrificing, but sometimes it was also their families who had to make sacrifices in the name of the war effort. In November a district commissioner of an unnamed county which had to watch over 100 miles of coastline described how he had obtained help from some scouts from Yorkshire. The boys had made a big difference but he related how one boy, who was about to go on his first leave, had a sorrowful expression.

When he asked what was wrong the boy answered that he loved the work and had put on a stone in weight since undertaking this duty but he was fearful he would not be able to return. This was because his mother had contacted him saying that she wanted the money which he had been earning down the pit before he had been posted. The commissioner told him that he must do as his mother instructed; he did, however, return in the end.

The same commissioner also told how one of his boys, a keen patrol leader aged just over 15, along with another scout, had been at their posts when at around 10 pm the nearby lifeboat received a call-out to a ketch in distress. The boys obtained permission to watch the launch of the lifeboat, but the coxswain realised he was one short and asked the patrol leader to jump in and lend a hand. The boy immediately did so. The lifeboat was out until 7 am and managed to rescue four men off the ketch and two from a boat. Upon their return, however, the coastguard station officer was very angry and threatened to send the boy home if the commissioner did not give him a dressing down because the scouts were supposed to obtain permission from the station officer before they got into any boat. The commissioner duly delivered his dressing down but admitted that his heart was not in it and he had only done it as the station officer had made it a condition of the boy being retained at the station.

The physical growth of the lad mentioned above was not unusual. Dr Aldous, the commissioner for Portsmouth, wrote of how he had tried to keep a record of the physical characteristics of the boys who were undertaking coastguard duties. He gave details of four scouts. Scout G.A. was 16 and gained 2st. 1lb in six months; patrol leader C.F., aged 14, gained 1½ inches in height in six weeks and put on muscle; patrol leader C.C., aged 14½, increased in height by the same amount and his chest expanded by 3 inches in just three months; patrol leader A.T., aged 14, increased by 2½ inches in height and gained in chest measurement and weight in two months. Another scout, aged 15 and from a very good home where he lived well, was asked upon his return from leave if he found a difference between the food on the station and the food at home. He replied that the food at the station was good plain food and that he had put on 9lb in weight and gained ½ inch in height in two weeks. Of another 14-year-old scout he wrote that he had arrived as a boy, but after six months had left as a well-built man. Indeed, the scout's younger brother asserted that when his brother arrived home unexpectedly on leave his mother had failed to recognise him thinking him 'some big sailor'.[6] Several other lads from the same troop had subsequently volunteered as they wished to grow as big as him.

In order to ensure that there was a steady supply of boys eager and willing to join the scouts it was considered essential to inculcate those too young to yet join with the spirit of the movement in order to build a desire to join when old enough. The Wolf Cubs were the successful means of doing just this. The cubs learned many of the basic scouting skills and their training was designed to encourage a desire for more knowledge. Sir Robert Baden-Powell worked alongside the Board of

Wolf Cubs salute the Mayor of Westminster. (The Sphere)

Above: *Wolf
Cubs learn the
arts of camping.*
(The Sphere)

Right: *Leeds
University Troop
practice fire drills.*
(Leeds Mercury)

Education to develop a curriculum for the cubs which would achieve the aims of developing intelligence, physical development, skills in handicraft, a desire to be of service to others and, most crucially, the desire to gain more knowledge. On 16 December 1916 the Wolf Cubs from Westminster gave an exhibition at Caxton Hall, Westminster. The guest of honour at the event was the Mayor of Westminster, Chief Scout for Westminster.

With the third wartime Christmas approaching, the press continued to report on the breadth of useful activities which were undertaken by the scouts across Britain. The Leeds University Troop, for example, took part in many activities common to scouts across the country including mounting an all-night guard to undertake any emergency duties. Their training for these duties included fire-fighting drills in the event of accident or enemy action. The Leeds University Troop was made up largely of boys who were employed at the university.

Military Service

We have already heard how the first quartermaster of the Dundee Scouts Defence Corps had left in January 1915 to take up a commission with the Northumberland Fusiliers. Like so many scout officers who volunteered, he did not survive the war. Aged just 19, Lieutenant Kenneth Stuart Hall died of wounds on 25 January 1916 while serving on attached duty to the 21st Division's mounted troops with the 21st Divisional Cyclist Company, Army Cyclist Corps. Lieutenant Hall was the son of Robert and Margaret Hall of 'Elmbank', Dollar, Clackmannanshire, and was a native of St Andrew's, Fife.[7]

The scouting ethos remained strong on the front-line and some former scouts even went so far as to form new troops with their own scoutmasters in the trenches. One unnamed regiment in France had a two-patrol troop formed within its ranks and the scoutmaster wrote home describing how, on St George's Day, the troop had paraded and retaken their promise in the field, worked at various scouting tests, attended an evening service and had finished the day off with their camp being bombed by a German aircraft before they went to bed.

Letters from former scouts almost universally praised the effect that the movement had upon the British Army in the field. One officer wrote home stating that he was almost constantly meeting former scouts and had been so impressed with the scouts that he decided that if he was not too old, when peace returned he would resign from his job and join the Boy Scout Association as a full-time officer.

In early March an impressive and well-attended service was held at Eastbourne's Holy Trinity Church to pay tribute to three former members of the Eastbourne scouts who had died at the front. One of these was Private W.H.E. Gallard of 2 Royal Sussex Regiment. Private Gallard had been killed on 12 January 1916 and was obviously well regarded locally as a number of family and friends attended the service (his father was serving at the front). During the service the continued good service of former scouts was praised, and current scouts were urged to follow the example of the three men.[8]

At the end of May 1916 the much-anticipated clash between the Royal Navy's Grand Fleet and the German High Fleet took place at Jutland. As the battle became more chaotic the light cruiser HMS *Cheshire* was sent to scout ahead of the 3rd Battlecruiser Squadron. Out of the haze emerged four German cruisers which began to fire upon the *Cheshire*. The gun-layer on one of the forward 5.5 inch guns was Boy 1st Class John Travers Cornwell. Known as Jack, the 16-year-old former scout was the sole survivor of his gun crew and, although very seriously wounded, remained at his post until *Cheshire* was able to retreat from the action. After the light cruiser made port, Cornwell was taken to Grimsby Hospital where he died on 2 June. For the incredible courage and dedication to duty which he displayed Jack Cornwell was awarded the Victoria Cross.

In the wake of the heroic sacrifice of Boy 1st Class John Travers (Jack) Cornwell, VC, the association acted quickly to inaugurate the

Cornwell Badge which was awarded for courage. The first 'Cornwell' scout was Edward Ireland, the leader of the scouts who were aboard the HMHS *Britannic*. The action of the boys in refusing to abandon ship until all the wounded had been evacuated was inspired by the actions of Ireland, who waited on the bridge with the captain, relaying the latter's orders until he was ordered off the bridge and taken below by a quartermaster. The captain later stated how pleased he had been with the conduct of Mr Ireland in remaining calm, even though he knew he was at risk of going down with the ship.

We have already heard how young Burton-on-Trent scout, Ronald Orme Crookes had been commissioned as a 2nd Lieutenant in 24 Royal Fusiliers. Sadly for this young man, aged just 18, he was to suffer the fate of so many young subalterns; he was killed in action on 4 June.[9]

At the beginning of June the lads of the Berwick Boy Scouts paraded at the headquarters of the county association. The event was to award no less than sixty of the boys with their war badges, earned by those who had given regular wartime service (mostly coast-watching). The duty was carried out by Major A. Steven and the Mayoress of Berwick.

HMHS Britannic. (Public Domain)

In front of the headquarters was a flagpole flying the Union Flag, while the scouts' flag flew from their tent. The parade was inspected and speeches made by a number of local dignitaries including the Mayor. The parade was led by the Berwick Boy Scouts Pipe Band led by Pipe Major Dumbreck and made for a splendid display, despite the rain. As Scoutmaster Clements was on military service the scouts were led by Scoutmaster E.W. Turnbull, ably assisted by Scoutmasters G.H. Ballard and Frank Moore, along with assistant Scoutmasters Bishop, Cowe, Dodds, Hall, Pickering and Renwick. Speeches were cut short because of the weather but included references to the beginnings of the scouting movement in Berwick when, in 1908, just seven boys left school and decided to form a troop. This quickly grew and their first camp was held in 1909 when eighteen or nineteen boys attended.[10] It was pointed out that of this original complement, six were now either captains or lieutenants in the army. The troop was divided into two patrols (Beaver and Wolf) and out of the nineteen boys in these patrols, ten were now serving at the front.

Original members of Berwick Boy Scouts Troop

Beaver Patrol	Wolf Patrol
David Stuart (patrol leader)	Alec C.A. Steven (patrol leader)
Thomas Hogarth (corporal)	Joseph Wright (corporal) (Scremerston)
G. Ferrier Steven (lance corporal)	J.D. Edminson (lance corporal)
N. Hunter (Milfield)	F. Seals
J. Hendry (Mordington)	J. Hogg (Beal)
Gordon Riddell	W. Gray (Edrington)
E. Gray	Eric Mackay
R. Hogarth	W. Prentice
P. Hendry (Mordington)	W. Hendry (Mordington)
A. Wright (Scremerston)	

The Berwick Boy Scouts Pipe Band. (The Berwickshire News)

Berwick seems to have been extremely proud of the activities of its scouts and the local press gave extensive coverage of their activities. Much of this coverage demonstrated how the movement was assisting the war effort while a significant proportion was dedicated to informing locals of how many former members had joined the forces and were at the front. In this manner the movement was serving as an additional and unofficial recruitment scheme which urged young men to join up and encouraged boys who were approaching military service age to fulfil their duty to their King and country. Indeed, the official march of the Boy Scouts was published in *The Berwickshire News* on several occasions. The rather jingoistic and simplistic lyrics demonstrated this recruitment aspect. They included, for example, the line, 'Boys, Mother England is calling to you ... join in our wonderful game'.

Among the patriotic activities of the Berwick Boy Scouts was the drawing-up of a roll of honour listing those scouts and former scouts who had served in the forces. Regular appeals appeared for families to provide details for this roll of honour and at the time of the above parade the first draft of this had just been published, on it were more than ninety names, five of whom were listed as having lost their lives in service.

The Boys Scouts March. (The Berwickshire News)

Berwick Boy Scouts 1st Roll of Honour

Rank	Name	Unit	Notes
Captain	A. Tower Robertson		County Commissioner
RQMS	R. Cooper Clements	Northumberland Fusiliers	Hon. Secretary & scoutmaster (Spittal)
Captain	H.R. Smail	NF	
Captain	A. Noel Smith	NF	
Lieutenant	J.A.T. Robertson	2/3 Queen Alexandra's Own Gurkha Rifles	Killed aboard SS Persia
Lieutenant	Alec C.A. Steven	Royal Engineers	
Lieutenant	G. Ferrier Steven	NF	
Lieutenant	Frank Weddell Smail	1/7 NF	Died of wounds
Lieutenant	F.B. Cowen	NF	
Lieutenant	Allan L. Trainer	London Regiment	
Lieutenant	Ian Mackay	Royal Field Artillery	
Lieutenant	R. Edminson	NF	
Captain	W.D. Reid	Dorset Regiment	
Lieutenant	Robert Paxton Reid	King's Own Scottish Borderers	
	John Reid		
	N. Ironside	Royal Scots	
	J. Ironside		
	Bertie Peters	1 Dorsets	
	L. Simmens	Black Watch	
	Edmund Smith	Royal Field Artillery	

	J. Campbell	NF	
	J. Jobson	NF	
	W.M. Dodds		
	G. Turnbull	NF	
	R. Scott	NF	
	William Russell		
	Gordon Riddell		
	Eric D. Mackay		
	T. Edminson	Army Service Corps	
	R. Knox	Machine Gun Corps	
	W. Austin	MGC	
	J. Weatherly	NF	
	W. Ormiston		
Sergeant	G. Evans	10 Canadian Infantry	Killed
	James Evans	NF	Killed
	Joseph Edminson	NF	
	A. Thompson	ASC	
	William Brown	RS	
	H. Dickinson	NF	
	H. Robertson	NF	
	G.S. Wilson	RS	
	J. Richardson	Royal Naval Air Service	
	D.A. Lamb	Scots Guards	
	S. Bell	Royal Flying Corps	
	John Hendry	4 KOSB	Killed
	William Hendry	4 KOSB	
	J. Skeldon	NF	
	Joseph Wright	Canadians	
	D. Wright	Canadians	

Rank	Name	Unit	Notes
Sergeant (cont'd)	H. Pearce		
	Walton	KOSB	
	E. Sinclair		
	A. Middlemiss	Black Watch	
	B. Hancock	NF	
	W. Miller	NF	
	J. McDonald	NF	
	J. Addison	NF	
	T. Hogarth	Lothian & Border Horse	
	J. Outterson	LBH	
	A. Gregson	9 Royal Scots	
	J.E. Boal	NF	
	E. Ogden	NF	
	J. Weatherhead	Royal Field Artillery	
	F. Lamb	ASC	
	J. McQueen	Royal Field Artillery	
	J. Lindsay	Highland Light Infantry	
	M. Anderson		
	W. Hardy	LBH	
	T. Davidson	LBH	
	R. Muir		
	G. Rutherford	NF	
	A. Martin	LBH	
	H. Morton	RN	
	Varner Russell		
	M. Alexander	Royal Field Artillery	

	James Forsyth	LBH	
	W. Brett	Royal Field Artillery	
	J. Barker	NF	
	B. Egan	NF	
	R. Attridge	NF	
	F. Seals	NF	
	A.L. Miller	Australians	
	Norman Elliott	YMCA Huts	
	Peter Renwick	YMCA Huts	
	Thomas Smart	4 Royal Scots	
	James Fairbarin		
	J. Bryson	NF	
	A. Smith	NF	
	A. Gladstone	NF	
	Thomas Hall	Royal Field Artillery	
	Thomas Lockhart	NF	
	George Crow	NF	

The opening of the Somme offensive on 1 July 1916 took a fearful toll of the British Army and several former scouts were among those who lost their lives on that day. Among them were Private Joseph Scott (21) from Colne in Lancashire. There is some confusion over which regiment Private Scott was serving in. The local press reported that he was serving with the Border Regiment, but the Commonwealth War Graves Commission has registered him as serving with 1 Royal Inniskilling Fusiliers. Before enlisting, Private Scott had worked as a weaver in his hometown and had connections with the St John Street Mission, as well as being an active member of the Boy Scouts troops associated with the mission.

The Battle of the Somme took its toll of former Berwick scouts. On 23 July Private G.S. Wilson, 9 Royal Scots, was killed during the fierce fighting for possession of Delville Wood. Like so many, Private

Wilson had joined up at the start of the war. He is buried at Delville Wood Cemetery.

One former scout to be awarded a medal for gallantry during the Battle of the Somme was Sergeant Harry Cator. Sergeant Cator was a native of Norfolk and had been a boy scout there. He worked for some time as a porter on the London Midland and Great Northern Joint Line before taking a job as a building contractor in Great Yarmouth. He enlisted in the East Surrey Regiment in September 1914 and was sent to France in 1915 as a Sergeant with the 7th Battalion. During the Somme Offensive Sergeant Cator went out to rescue thirty-six wounded men who were lying in no man's land. For his courage in doing so he was awarded with the Military Medal (although he did not actually receive the medal until August 1917).

At 100 Springfield Road, Burnley, Charles and Tamar Jordan received the telegram that was feared across Britain. It told them that their son, Private William Robert Jordan, had been killed in action at the front. Private Jordan was formerly a patrol leader with the St Stephen's Troop and had worked as a weaver. He had joined the army and had come through the Battle of Loos without any harm, but on 5 July he had been wounded in the thigh; following treatment at a

base hospital he had been posted back to the front with 10 Cameronians (Scottish Rifles), only to be killed on 28 August.

As the Battle of the Somme rumbled on casualties continued to be high, with September being a particularly bad month. On 15 September the British Army pioneered the use of tanks at the Battle of Flers-Courcelette. The British attack succeeded in taking the village of Flers, but at a heavy cost. Among those to be killed in this attack was Rifleman Thomas Rowland Prime of 18 King's Royal Rifle Corps. Rifleman Rowland was a former scout who had lived with a relative

Private W.R. Jordan.
(Burnley News)

in Belper in Derbyshire because both his parents were dead. The young man threw himself into the scouting movement, being one of the first to join the Belper Troop where he served as a bugler. In June 1915 he enlisted following a stirring appeal made at a local Red Cross hospital by the district commissioner. Rifleman Prime left behind a sister, Emma, and two half-sisters.[11] There was some confusion over the loss of Rifleman Prime as the local press reported his surname as being Prince, but this appears to have been an error. With the confusion of combat and the sheer number of casualties, the army's system of notification was almost at breaking point at this stage of the war and there were many instances of confusion. The loss of Rifleman Prime was one of them, with his sister not being officially notified of his death until 3 November. Before this she had been informed by a comrade of her brother that Rifleman Prime had been wounded.

Rifleman Prime. (Belper News and Derbyshire Telephone)

On the day following the death of Rifleman Prime yet another former member of the scouts was killed in action. Private Clive R. Sears was killed while serving with 13 King's (Liverpool Regiment), he had been at the front only a short time. Before the war, Private Sears had been a keen member of his local Sea Scouts troop. He is commemorated on the Thiepval Memorial.

On 25 September, Private John Peer Flanders of 8 Leicestershire Regiment was killed in action aged 21. Before the war Private Flanders had lived at Beaconsfield Cottage in Quorn and was apprenticed to a Leicester firm of bicycle makers. He had been a keen member of the Boy Scouts and was a patrol

Private Clive R. Sears. (Liverpool Echo)

leader in the BP Scouts Troop. In 1913 he had been one of the attendees at the large scout rally held in Birmingham. Private Flanders was a keen and talented boxer and won the 9 stone Leicestershire championship, reaching the final of the Boy Scouts boxing competition, where he was beaten. Like so many who fell at the Somme, Private Flanders has no known grave and is commemorated on the Thiepval Memorial.

Just four months after he was mentioned in the roll of honour Captain Alexander Noel Smith (20), 7 Northumberland Fusiliers, died of wounds sustained in action on 26 September.

Among the former scouts to be killed in October was Sapper Arthur Topham of the 84th Field Company, Royal Engineers. Arthur was another Boy Scout who had enlisted young, aged just 18. Before the war he had been employed as a tubing smith at the M.R. Locomotive Works. He had been at the front for some sixteen months before his death on 7 October.[12]

Lance Corporal John Muirhead of Armadale, West Lothian, had been a keen follower of the Boy Scouts movement and had been an officer of the local scouts when, like so many, he joined up at the very beginning of the war. Muirhead had joined the Scots Guards where he had befriended two other former Armadale scouts, Matthew Campbell and Robert Darling. In early 1915 Muirhead had been badly wounded in the back and it was while at home recuperating that he heard that Private Matthew Campbell, who had enlisted with him, had been killed in action during the Battle of Loos.[13] After returning to his unit Lance Corporal Muirhead was awarded the Military Medal in April 1916. By the summer of that year the two comrades found themselves thrown into the hellish Battle of the Somme and Private Robert Darling (24) was killed on 15 September.[14] After this further personal loss, Muirhead (24) was granted a period of welcome leave and returned to his hometown. During his leave he was honoured at Armadale Town Hall by the local people before he returned to his unit. At the end of November Muirhead's sweetheart, who was working in London, encountered one of Muirhead's chums and was given the awful news that, on 15 November, Muirhead and another soldier had gone out into no-mans land to look for their captain and Muirhead had been shot and killed by a sniper. Muirhead's sweetheart immediately got permission to visit home and was surprised to find that Muirhead's parents had not yet been officially notified. The official notification arrived days later, and the news reportedly caused sadness across Armadale where Lance Corproal Muirhead was recognised as being a fine young man.[15]

It was not only in the army that former scouts were serving. Many had joined the ranks of the Royal Navy. Many of these boys had decided upon this while serving as coast watchers shortly after the beginning of the war. At the start of the war the Admiralty had commandeered a large number of vessels, many of them from the fishing industry, for service as minesweepers. This was a hugely dangerous task and many men lost their lives while engaged in sweeping the seas for these threats. One of the commandeered vessels was the drifter *Michaelmas Daisy* which had been built at Aberdeen in 1913 and which was fishing out of Lowestoft. Converted to minesweeping duties and renamed HM Drifter *Michaelmas Daisy* in 1914, the little boat served for two years. On 26 November the little ship was off Cap St Maria di Leuca (Italy) when it struck a mine and was sunk with the loss of all twelve crewmen. Among them was Deck Boy Wilfred Leslie Burrows who was aged just 17 and from Taunton. Wilfred was described as a very bright boy and was a keen member of the St Mary's Troop, which he had belonged to for several years. At the start of the war he had been one of the lads who had volunteered to serve as an aid to the Coastguard in Cornwall. In May 1915, aged 16, he enlisted in the Royal Navy as a signal boy. For some time he served aboard a minesweeper which was patrolling off the south coast before he was posted abroad. At the end of 1915 he had been given leave and had entertained family and friends with his tales. Wilfred wrote many letters home to his father and in the last one he seemed cheerful. Sadly, his father had only just sent off a Christmas present for his only son. The Burrows family situation was particularly tragic as his father was bedridden with an illness and his mother had recently died.[16]

Deck Boy Wilfred Leslie Burrows. (The Courier)

The courage of many of the former Boy Scouts who served is made clear by numerous mentions of awards throughout the war. On 14 December one such man, Sergeant Harold Chismall (20) of the King's (Liverpool Regiment), was praised in his hometown of Ormskirk for his courage. Sergeant Chismall had been awarded the Distinguished Conduct Medal, the Military Medal and the Russian Order of St George. Upon spending leave at home the former member of an Ormskirk troop was awarded a silver wrist watch and money by the Ormskirk Scouts. Thankfully, it appears that Sergeant Chismall survived the war.

CHAPTER 4

1917

Home Front

New Year's Day in Berwick featured the presentation of a medal to patrol leader George Hawkins. The award was made following the rescue of a young lad from the River Tweed by Hawkins in August of the previous year. Patrol Leader Hawkins was an enthusiastic and skilled scout who had a reputation for his swimming ability, having been trained in swimming and rescue work. He belonged to 3 Berwick Troop and was known as a very enthusiastic scout who had attended numerous camps and performed wartime coast-watch service at Berwick Coastguard Station. On the day in question, Hawkins had witnessed a young boy named Marshall (aged 7 or 8) fall from one of the jetties at Berwick Quay into the Tweed. Hawkins had immediately stripped off and jumped in to rescue the drowning boy.

A large number of boys attended the ceremony at the Town Hall. The Mayor and Mayoress were both present along with Surgeon Major Mackay and Major Robertson. Dr Mackay made a speech in which he paid testimony to the bravery which Hawkins had displayed, and talked of the gallantry that the Berwick Boy Scouts had demonstrated thus far during the war. He also remarked that the events of the previous August should act as a stimulus to all the lads there of the importance of learning to swim.

Following the award of the medal Major Tower Robertson proposed a vote of thanks during which he fulsomely praised Hawkins' scoutmaster, Mr Turnbull, saying that he put everything into his involvement with the scouts. He also praised the character of the local boys who made up the Berwick scouts. In reply Major Mackay added that he had no fear of

Patrol leader Hawkins.
(Berwickshire News)

the future given that they had boys such as Hawkins and his fellow scouts in their community.

The sight of the Boy Scout uniform became a familiar one during the war. Now with the war in its third year, and with the growing sense of weariness at ever-increasing casualty figures, it is creditable that the organisation seemed to maintain the morale of its members. One of the more unusual sights was that of the 5th Brockley Scouts. This south London troop had a strong link with the London Scottish Regiment and its members therefore paraded in kilts of Forbes tartan. By June, the 5th Brockley had grown to 120 members and included six pipers and four drummers, as well as a bulldog mascot named John. The 5th Brockley had undertaken many tasks in aid of the war effort, the police and the municipal authorities, functioning as messengers, first-aiders as well as other tasks. This was reflected in the large number of badges worn by the boys, including seventy War Badges earned for such tasks. A large number of the troop had become King's Scouts having been recognised as a First Class Scout (having passed ten tests) alongside the achievement of a further four badges from a list of seven, one of which had to be the Pathfinder badge.

On 20 April there was a meeting in Newcastle-upon-Tyne which discussed the future of the Boy Scouts movement in both Newcastle and Northumberland. Due to his military service the district commissioner, the Duke of Northumberland, was unable to attend and his place as chair was taken by Captain Alexander Leith, MC. In the necessary preamble Captain Leith stated that it was the duty of the movement to 'improve the rising generation, the Empire's future manhood'. For some time there had been concern that many young boys in Newcastle were

LONDON BOYS WHO WEAR THE KILT AND FOLLOW THE PIPES: THE 5TH BROCKLEY SCOUTS SETTING OUT TO CHURCH PARADE LAST SUNDAY

The Care for the Rising Generation

BROCKLEY is doing admirably with its Scouts, who are about 120 strong, have six pipers, with four drummers and wear Forbes tartan. They have been much utilised by the municipal and police authorities. Their mascot is a bulldog called "John." Most of the boys can show many Scout badges. About seventy now wear the War Badge, and a large number are King's Scouts.

FEW comparatively of the general public are aware of the excellent adjunct of the work of the National Refuges for Homeless and Destitute Children, 164, Shaftesbury Avenue, London, W.C. 2, which is to be found in the Fordham House Working Boys' Home. There are many mothers who have not the accommodation at home for the lads who have finished their training in the Country Homes, nor are they in a position to assist them in securing good employment. By a wise provision the committee are able to look after such lads and to see that they are placed in situations which may lead them to become skilled workmen, or able to fill positions of trust. Truly a work making for good citizens in the days to come. It is asking for help.

MISS GLADYS ANDERSON, with four friends—Miss Winifred Saunders, Miss Winifred Rose, Miss Lavinia Caston and Miss Maun Ewin—is doing excellent work in entertaining large military hospitals and camps.

Miss GLADYS ANDERSON   MRS. E. B. BURKE

CAPTAIN EDWARD BERNARD BURKE, King's Own Regiment, grandson of Sir Bernard Burke, C.B., Ulster King of Arms, was married on June 2 to Eileen, daughter of Mr. Justin M'Carthy, Ard-na-bel, Co. Dublin.

The Education of the Illustrator

A NEW art series is appearing in the shape of "The Art of the Illustrator," by Percy V. Bradshaw, and issued by the Press Art School, Tudor Hall, Forest Hill, London, of which he is director. It represents a scheme by which the methods of various artists are set forth, together with reproductions of some of their illustrations in various stages of completion. Twenty artists will be dealt with, of whom twelve have so far been presented, including Lawson Wood, F. Matania, Bert Thomas, W. Heath Robinson, W. Russell Flint, R.W.S., Charles E. Brock, R.I., F. H. Townsend, Harry Rountree, Claude A. Shepperson, A.R.W.S., Frank Reynolds, R.I., Spencer Pryse and the late Cyrus Cuneo, R.I. Each section is made up as a folio portfolio, the text being in a section by itself, and the (six) stages of the drawing selected being mounted on grey boards. The idea is excellent. The entire work (of twenty parts) costs seven guineas, separate sections costing 10s. 6d. each.

THE directors of Carreras, Limited, have declared an interim dividend on the ordinary shares at the rate of 8 per cent. for the half-year ended April 30.

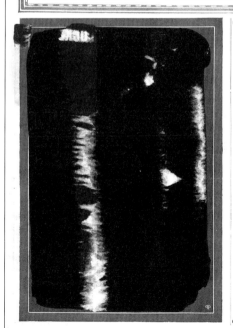

5th Brockley Boy Scouts with pipers, drummers and mascot (The Graphic)

becoming involved in activities which were not necessarily wholesome, and the Home Office had contacted the Lord Mayor of Newcastle to ask if some organisation could be created to ensure that the 'boys and youths of the city might be trained and guided to become useful members of society and helpful citizens of our Empire'.[1] The Lord Mayor had approached the Northumberland Boy Scouts Association, who had given the matter lengthy consideration.

As a result of the above, the General Purposes Committee of the Northumberland Boy Scouts Association had decided that the formation of a large boys' club would be the best approach. Mr Rainbow of the Northern Command Cross-Country Committee had volunteered his services in the running of such a club and he, together with Mr F.F. Corballis (the assistant district commissioner) and the Lord Mayor, had identified a suitable large site which was in one of the more crowded parts of the city. The building would easily house 700 boys and would be suitable for games, exercises, reading and working, but would require a very significant capital outlay. The scheme, however, had to be abandoned for the present because Mr Rainbow had recently had to withdraw; the ranks of his workers were being rapidly denuded by the demands of military and national service and he could no longer guarantee suitable supervision of the club during the evenings.

The matter was not helped by the fact that the Northumberland Boy Scout Association was not very well organised and Captain Leith asked for help in putting the association on a good footing. If this was done, he believed, the association would be able to deliver what the Home Office and Lord Mayor were asking of them. In order to do this, Captain Leith had spoken with the various local officers and they had decided that the only course of action was to centralise the organisation. He therefore proposed that a central committee be formed with the city and county working together. This central committee would be formed of thirty members, fifteen from the city and fifteen from the county. The biggest problem was, unsurprisingly, money, and Captain Leith estimated that a public appeal for some £10,000 must be made. The association was to get a fresh start. Captain Leith revealed that His Grace the Duke of Northumberland had offered to resign owing to his military duties, but the Chief Scout had asked him to continue. Now, His Grace had once again offered to resign and this time he was accepted. His suggestion of Mr Corballis taking over from him had met with hearty approval as Mr Corballis had been largely responsible for the wartime revival of the movement in Northumberland.

By the summer of 1917 the air raid was a source of fear for many across the country, but especially in London. A series of raids saw several squadrons of the RFC withdrawn from France to provide additional protection to the capital. Many scouts played an active and danger-filled role in these air raids. Scouts acted as guides to the few rudimentary shelters and as buglers who sounded alerts in some areas when an air raid was detected. These activities clearly placed them at great risk during the raids but Sir Robert Baden-Powell could illuminate the movement with his own, albeit limited, experience of an air raid. At Hurlingham in July he addressed a rally of over 1,500 scouts from south-west London. Sir Robert used the event to explain how he had recently been on a journey to address a similar meeting when his train was hit by a bomb and several people were killed or injured. Explaining how he had gone to the aid of one man who had suffered a badly gashed leg, he had been beaten to the casualty by another man. When he asked if he could be of assistance, the other man gave him the scout sign. This, Sir Robert, declared was a typical example of a scout in action and Sir Robert declared just how pleased he was to see so many scouts with proficiency badges indicating their wartime service.

In August there was a tragedy involving the Northumberland Boy Scouts. Senior Patrol Leader Thomas Geddes Morpeth (17) of the Wallsend Association lived at 13 Laburnum Avenue, Wallsend, and was an apprentice engineer. The son of a local councillor, the patrol leader was a King's Scout and was instructing a squad of junior scouts when he accidentally met his death. On 11 August, Patrol Leader Morpeth, a leader in the St Luke's Troop, had completed drilling his young charges when someone suggested they should have some climbing practice. Thomas got a rope secured to a chimney and one of the boys climbed up and down. Thomas then said he would go next, but as he was descending the chimney gave way and he fell to the ground striking his head. He was taken home bleeding from wounds to the back of the head and his right forehead. Thomas was taken to hospital but subsequently died of his injuries.

His funeral was very well attended. Not only were his family and friends present, but also 279 Wallsend scouts under the district scoutmaster, Mr McKeith, while the Newcastle Association sent forty scouts under Assistant Scoutmaster Sudwicks of the 19th Troop. Also present were several officers of the Wallsend and Newcastle associations. Wreaths were sent from each of the seven Wallsend troops, by the commissioner of Wallsend, from Scoutmaster Morpeth's work colleagues in Wallsend, the lady munitions workers from Parson's Works, from his foremen and from several scouts.

On 10 September, the boy scouts of Hull suffered a tragic loss when 10-year-old George Albert Thomas of Magdala Road died in hospital. Several weeks previously the boy had been playing with friends when he threw a hockey ball at a wall. The ball rebounded and hit George on the right ear. After the ear became discoloured and began discharging fluid, and with the boy complaining of headaches, he was treated as an out-patient at the city's Great Northern Hospital. Unfortunately, the lad's condition worsened, and he died shortly after being admitted to the hospital. The subsequent inquest into the death determined that George had died of acute meningitis following inflammation of the middle ear, accelerated by the blow from the hockey ball. The jury subsequently returned a verdict of accidental death.

At the end of October a further air raid hit south-west London, killing six. Among the fatalities during this raid was a boy scout. Alfred Page (13) was one of those scouts who had volunteered as a bugler in the event of air raids and he was in his house with his father, waiting for the order to sound the all-clear, when a bomb fell on the property and killed both Mr Page and his son. His mother and two younger siblings, along with several others, were saved as they had taken shelter in an ad-hoc bunker made from furniture on the ground floor. Alfred was described by his teachers as 'a splendid little fellow', who was popular and a fine pupil of whom much was expected.[2] Alfred's death made national headlines and newspapers across the country covered the death of the scout in some detail. The *Dundee Evening Telegraph*, for example, called Alfred 'a ripping little chap', and described how everyone was singing the praises of the young scout who had 'died serving his country as faithfully as any man'.[3] The article went on to explain that Alfred had been found dead alongside his father and was dressed in his uniform with bugle in hand as he awaited the order to sound the all-clear.

The activities of the Boy Scouts during this series of air raids on the capital drew much attention and praise and the movement was keen to promote them and to recognise the bravery of scouts. A raid that had hit Poplar saw several Boy Scouts honoured. An air ace from the RFC inspected an assembly of scouts at St Matthias Church and presented a flag and several certificates. At the same parade, Sir Robert Baden-Powell presented three scouts with framed certificates for their gallant work during the raid. The buglers of the Boy Scouts who served through air raids had been taken to the hearts of the people of London and the boys were given pride of place (second only to two tanks) in the 1917 Lord Mayor's Parade.

Although the Lord Mayor's Parade was one of the grandest examples, the morale of the scouts was maintained throughout the war by constant parades, inspections and gatherings which served not only to encourage greater membership, but also to highlight the work which was being done by the movement. These gatherings, both large and small, were often overseen and inspections taken by military officers of local standing. In October a gathering of 750 Boy Scouts and Girl Guides took place at Foots Cray Place, Kent. The inspecting officer on this occasion was Brigadier General E.B. Applebee.

Scoutmaster Allen is presented with flag at Poplar. (Daily Mirror)

Poplar Boy Scout being presented with medal. (Daily Mirror)

The Lord Mayor's Parade at the Mansion House. (The Sphere)

The rally of Boy Scouts and Girl Guides at Foots Cray Place, Kent. (The Tatler)

The contribution of the Boy Scouts Association to the war effort was, as we have seen, very considerable indeed, and it did not go unappreciated. In 1917 the Prime Minister stated:

I do not think I am exaggerating when I say that the young boyhood of our country, represented by the Boy Scouts Association, shares the laurels for having been prepared with the old and trusted and tried British Army and Navy. For both proved their title to make the claim when the Great War broke upon us like a thief in the night. It is no small matter to be proud of that the Association was able within a month of the outbreak of war to give the most energetic and intelligent help in all kinds of service. When the boyhood of a nation can give such practical proofs of its honour, straightness and loyalty, there is not much danger of that nation going under, for these boys are in training to render service to their country as leaders in all walks of life in the future.[4]

Naturally, the movement made great play of such testimonials and used them to encourage more boys to join. It was also at pains to point out that although the movement was training boys to 'render service to their country', it was not a military organisation. The association made the argument that the drill being practised was more comparable to that which enabled schoolchildren to move around in groups than the military version, and that 'the idea of compulsory discipline ... was so foreign as to be almost antagonistic to the first principle of scouting'.[5]

One of the reasons which enabled the scouts to adapt to the wide variety of tasks which they undertook during the war was that the organisational simplicity of the movement (compared to the British Army and Royal Navy) allowed it to be endlessly and speedily adaptable to a wide variety of demands.

Military Service

1917 began with bitter news for the family and friends of Lance Corporal W.F.B. Finney of Bakewell. The young soldier was a former member of the local Church Lads' Brigade as well as the local troop of Boy Scouts, and had enlisted in the Derbyshire Yeomanry at the outbreak of the war. When this regiment was sent to France, Finney had found himself posted to 14 Durham Light Infantry and it was while serving with the battalion that he was shot and killed by a sniper on 7 January. His sister, Mrs B. Thompson of King Street, Bakewell, received a letter from a Captain Allden Owles just two days following her brother's death (Lance Corporal Finney's parents were both deceased). The letter described how Lance Corporal Finney had been shot and killed by the sniper despite medical attempts to save him, and expressed the sorrow of both Captain Owles and his men over the death of a soldier who he described as ever-willing, dependable and well respected by both officers and men, before reassuring Mrs Thompson that her brother had been buried in a nearby cemetery with a military funeral and that a cross was soon to be erected over the grave.[6]

On 11 April, yet another of those Berwick Scouts who had been named on the very first roll of honour in the local newspaper was killed in action. Private Richard Scott was aged just 20 when he was killed with 22 (Tyneside Scottish) Northumberland Fusiliers. Richard was a native of Berwick and his parents, Richard and Elizabeth, received word of their son's death at their home at 7 Church Street, Berwick-upon-Tweed.[7]

The Irish section of the Boy Scouts Association suffered a terrible loss when its former secretary was killed in action in Mesopotamia on 15 April. Hedley W. Craig was a native of Wicklow and had attended Aravon School, Bray; St Stephen's Green School and Trinity College, Dublin. He was a keen athlete and as part of the university's harriers took part in many races. He won several at distances of between 440 yards and two miles and in 1910, 1911 and 1912, had finished runner-up in the All-Irish Half Mile Championship and runner-up in the Irish Inter-Varsity Championship of 1912, at both mile and half mile. In addition to his activities with the Boy Scouts and athletics, Hedley also had a strong faith and served as Superintendent of the Fishamble Street Mission. He had been about to take up a divinity course when war broke out. In September 1914 he enlisted as a motor dispatch rider before being gazetted as an officer in the Royal Engineers in January 1916. In May of that year he was posted to Mesopotamia and attached to the Royal Flying Corps which posted him to 30 Squadron as an observer/gunner, flying the outdated BE2c reconnaissance aircraft. On 15 April, 2nd Lieutenant Craig and his pilot, Captain Charles Leigh Pickering, were carrying out a reconnaissance flight over Basra when they were attacked and shot down by Hauptmann Hans Schuz in his Halberstadt fighter aircraft. Both RFC men were killed. Hauptmann Schuz carried out the funeral service personally and arranged for the graves of the two RFC men to be marked with the broken propeller from their aircraft.[8]

On the night of 20/21 April, six German destroyers bombarded Calais while another six bombarded Dover just before midnight. Early the next morning two British destroyers, HMS *Broke* and HMS *Swift*, located the Dover group and, despite being outnumbered, engaged the enemy. What became known as the Second Battle of the Dover Straits was a confused action in which HMS *Swift* successfully sank a German destroyer while HMS *Broke* rammed another. The two destroyers became locked together and the German crew attempted to board the British vessel, resulting in hand-to-hand fighting. The Germans were

The original graves of Captain Pickering and Lieutenant Craig. (Public Domain)

repulsed, the two ships separated and HMS *Broke* sank its adversary, despite itself suffering heavy damage which necessitated the destroyer having to be towed back to port. From that engagement came yet another former Boy Scout hero. Midshipman Donald Allan Gyles was stationed on the forecastle of HMS *Broke* and had already helped the depleted forward gun-crews reload their guns, but had been wounded in the eye. When the German boarding party tried to storm the ship he blocked their path alone, despite being half blinded, and held them long enough for reinforcements to arrive. Midshipman Gyles was a native of Muswell Hill and had gone through the Gallipoli campaign where he had been wounded at Gaba Tepe. For his courage, Midshipman Gyles was awarded the Distinguished Service Cross.[9]

April 1917 witnessed the horrific Arras offensive. The battles near Arras took the lives of many former scouts, while others were rewarded for their immense courage under fire during the fighting. Among these was yet another scout VC. We have already heard how Sergeant Harry Cator had earned the MM on the Somme in 1916. On 9 April Sergeant Cator was in action at Arras; while advancing over open ground, Sergeant Cator's platoon had taken heavy casualties from an enemy machine gun. In an effort to get the attack moving forward once more, Sergeant Cator and another soldier took a Lewis Gun forward. When the other soldier was killed, Sergeant Cator took the gun and

HMS Broke.
(Public Domain)

Damage to HMS Broke under repair on Tyneside. (Tyne & Wear Archives & Museums)

charged the enemy position. He knocked out one machine gun on the way and when he reached the German trench he spotted and attacked another machine gun position. He killed the entire machine gun team and their officer and held the trench to allow a bombing (grenade) team to capture 100 prisoners and five machine guns. A few days after this he was wounded when a shell exploded nearby. He was subsequently evacuated to recover at Beaufort Hospital in Bristol; while there, he heard of the award of not only the Victoria Cross, but also the French Croix de Guerre. On Friday 24 August he was still in hospital and was invited to a ceremony at the Council House in Bristol. The ceremony was attended by a large

Midshipman Gyles. (The Sketch)

number of well-wishers and dignitaries, including the Duchess of Beaufort, the Lady Mayoress, and the Bishop of Bristol. At the ceremony the Lady Mayoress pinned on Sergeant Cator's MM and CdG, as well as presenting him with an envelope saying that its contents might come in handy later. Sergeant Cator made a short speech thanking the people of Bristol for the kindness they had shown him and the soldiers who were fighting for them. Upon his return to the hospital Sergeant Cator was met at the train station by a large contingent of his wounded comrades (in their blue and red, wounded, uniforms) who picked him up and carried him on their shoulders to a waiting car. When he arrived back at hospital a band played 'See the Conquering Hero Comes', and a special supper followed. During this supper Sergeant Hain gave a short speech which he concluded by saying: 'Boys, I don't want to go back, you don't want to go back, but if we go we'll go back as Britishers. We are winning now, boys, and Germany knows it, and we who are recently back from the front know it.'[10]

Reginald Leonard Haine had previously been a King's Scout with the Petersham Troop and was a very keen and able boy scout. By April 1917 he was serving as a 2nd Lieutenant in the Honourable Artillery Company. He had joined the HAC as a Private at the very outset of the war and was, by now, a very experienced soldier of the

Sergeant Harry Cator,
VC, MM, CdG, in his
'wounded' uniform.
(Western Daily Press)

Western Front. On the night of 28/29 April he was one of a number of British soldiers holding a salient near to Gavrelle and was facing repeated German counter-attacks; 2nd Lieutenant Haine organised a group of men and led them in six grenade attacks on a German strong point. He and his men successfully captured the position along with fifty prisoners and two machine guns. The enemy immediately counter-attacked and managed to recapture the lost ground but 2nd Lieutenant Haine organised a block in his trench and occupied the position for the rest of the night. His citation for the Victoria Cross remarked on the remarkable example he had set to his men during thirty hours of continuous fighting.[11]

The scouting movement in Derbyshire was saddened to hear of the death of yet another member in April. Aged 15, Bernard Cyril Staniland Dixon had joined the Derby (Leander) Troop in 1912 and had quickly shown himself to be an enthusiastic and skilled scout, later being made assistant scoutmaster. He was a good athlete and was noted as being a particularly strong swimmer. He won a number of trophies and other awards for his swimming ability during his time with the troop and was noted as being a cheerful and bright young man. Bernard enlisted in the 1/6 Sherwood Foresters (Notts and Derby Regiment) but was killed in action during an attack mounted on 23 April (aged 20) and is commemorated on the Arras Memorial.

Another Derbyshire scout and member of 1/6 Sherwood Foresters was also killed in the same action as Private Dixon. In a letter to Private John Thomas Mather's parents, his company commander described how the attack had successfully driven the Germans from a group of houses and the Sherwood Foresters had set up a hasty defensive position to repel an expected counter-attack. Private Mather had been part of a Lewis Gun team and was posted in a very dangerous but crucial defensive position. The gun team performed fine work and killed a number of attacking German troops, but Private Mather was killed by return fire from a German machine gun. Private Mather had been with the BEF for twenty-six months and had only recently joined the Lewis Gun team. His commanding officer explained how Private Mather was widely respected by the men of the company, especially by those of his own No.2 Platoon. Before the war Private Mather had been assistant scoutmaster of the Unstone Troop and had worked for the Staveley Coal and Iron Company; he had joined the Territorials in July 1914 as war appeared likely. Described as a quiet and well-behaved lad, he was well liked in his home in the Derbyshire hamlet of Hundall.[12]

On 5 June yet another former boy scout earned the Victoria Cross. John Manson Craig was a native of Comrie, Perthshire, and had been educated at Crieff, where he had been a lieutenant in the school cadet corps before joining the army as a private in 1915. He had fought throughout the Battle of Loos before returning home to be commissioned as a 2nd lieutenant in the Royal Scots Fusiliers. On 5 June, 21-year-old Craig was serving at Gaza. On the day in question, an advanced post in front of his position had been attacked and overrun; 2nd Lieutenant Craig quickly organised a rescue party and led a successful counter-attack. During this attack a sergeant was wounded, and when a medical officer went out to him he too was wounded. Both men were lying in the open and were being fired upon; 2nd Lieutenant Craig immediately went out alone and managed to drag the sergeant to cover. He then went back for the medical officer but in dragging him back was himself wounded. He picked

Private John Thomas Mather.
(Derbyshire Courier)

himself up and managed to get the officer to cover, whereupon Craig immediately began to dig out further cover for the wounded men.

With the awful attrition of the fighting now causing an ever-increasing sense of war-weariness, it was vital that morale be maintained. In July the *Belper News* carried a story about Rifleman J.H. Taylor being awarded the Military Medal. A former member of Belper Troop, the young rifleman had joined up in 1915, aged 18, and was posted to the King's Royal Rifles. Like many scouts of the time, Rifleman Taylor had

2nd Lieutenant John Manson Craig, VC. (Public Domain)

a strong Christian upbringing and had been a choirboy at St Mark's in Openwoodgate. He clearly had taken the lessons taught as a scout to heart and he wrote home to say that what he had learned in the scouts had stood him in excellent stead for army service, with the discipline and knowledge he had obtained proving of great value. In return, the local scouts expressed their own excitement and pride at the military success of a former member. Rifleman Taylor wrote home describing the ceremony at which he had been presented his MM by a General in front of 3,000 troops and how he, along with other medal winners, had been saluted by the parade. The award of the MM to Rifleman Taylor had been for his courage in carrying dispatches while under heavy fire.[13]

Rifleman Taylor, MM. (Belper News)

Many former scouts went on to gain a commission and the battles and trench warfare on the Western Front took a dreadful toll on them. Frank Lane had been a scout with the 1st Ramsgate (General Sir Charles Warren's Own) Troop before joining up with the 17 London Regiment. On 16 May he was killed while serving as a 2nd Lieutenant attached to the 2/1 London Regiment.[14] 2nd Lieutenant C.H. Lee had formerly been scoutmaster of the 2nd Parkstone (Lady Baden-Powell's Own) Troop, but was serving with the 249th Siege Battery of the Royal Garrison Artillery when he was killed in action on 20 September.[15] Captain Charles Francis Bower (26) was former scoutmaster of the 1st Norwich Troop and was killed in action on 13 September while serving with 16 Sherwood Foresters (Notts and Derby Regt). Captain Bower was from Norwich and is buried at La Clytte Military Cemetery. 2nd Lieutenant L.W. Bowden Russell had been cubmaster of the 1st Tooting (St Peter's) Troop and was killed in action serving with 12 East Surrey Regiment.[16] 2nd Lieutenant Leslie Wallace Ablett was formerly a patrol leader in the 1st Streatham Troop but was killed in action while serving with 11 Northumberland Fusiliers on 15 October and is commemorated on the Tyne Cot Memorial. The scouting movement had, of course, spread well beyond Britain and it had found particularly fertile soil in many of the colonies. The Canadian and South African movements were particularly popular; on 12 October, former South African scout 2nd Lieutenant William Robert Hamilton, previously a member of the 2nd Capetown Troop, was killed in action. Having first served with the Coldstream Guards, by the time of his death Hamilton (26) was attached to 4th Company, Machine Gun Guards.[17]

It is unsurprising that these men joined up. The scouts created a body of young men and boys who had been brought up with an extremely well-developed sense of duty to King and country which was taught alongside a strongly militaristic regimen of training. Many former scouts had been influenced strongly enough to choose a career in the British Army or Royal Navy even before the war. Others had decided to follow this career during the early years of the war. Hugh Price Rose was brought up at Grosvenor Place, Newcastle upon Tyne, and had been educated at Sherbourne and Oriel College, Oxford, before attending Sandhurst. Rose (20), who was an only child, was killed in action as a 2nd Lieutenant in 2 Seaforth Highlanders on 11 April when the 9th (Scottish) Division attacked the village of Roeux. The village was constructed on a cave network which had been heavily fortified, and this initial attack failed.[18]

The war brought about many technical innovations and one which most excited many young men was that of flying. Aerial warfare had developed massively and by 1917, and despite an official policy of not naming them, the names of the aces (those who had scored more than five aerial victories) were becoming well known and romanticised. The reality was, of course, somewhat different and there was little romantic about the war in the air. Serving in the Royal Flying Corps or the Royal Naval Air Service was one of the most dangerous duties during the war. Frank Edward Winser, brought up in Tooting and a patrol leader in the 1st Tooting (St Peter's) Troop, had obviously been attracted by the glamour of flight. By 1917, aged just 19, he was serving with the RFC as a 2nd Lieutenant in France posted to 43 Squadron, which was flying fighter-reconnaissance sorties with the obsolescent Sopwith 1½ Strutter. Casualties in units operating this machine were very high, and on 20 August, 2nd Lieutenant Winser was killed in action.[19]

Not every young man who dreamt of going to war in the air saw his dream come to fruition; accidents during training took a horrific toll of lives throughout the war. 2nd Lieutenant James Stevenson had formerly been a patrol leader in the 2nd Orkney Troop. Known as an exceptionally bright and keen young man who had been enthusiastic in all his undertakings, James had ambitions to become a teacher, but eager to do his bit, he joined the RFC and graduated as a pilot in record time. Shortly before his death, he wrote home to a friend describing how, having gained his wings, he was now at an aerial gunnery school learning the art of deflection shooting in the air. This was at 2 (Auxiliary) School of Aerial Gunnery at Turnberry in Ayrshire. On 1 May he was detailed for a training flight in an FE2b (6975) with Sergeant Christopher William Henry Bowers as his pilot.[20] Upon approach to land at Turnberry the FE was seen to go into a sharp turn before losing flying speed and nose diving into the ground from 30ft.

A Sopwith 1½ Strutter of the RFC. (Public Domain)

A court of inquiry found that the sharp turn led the aircraft to lose speed and stall, causing the crash which killed both crewmen. Interestingly, the court also recommended that better medical facilities were required at Turnberry. 2nd Lieutenant Stevenson's funeral took place in his hometown and was attended by a large number of mourners, including a large number of scouts from his former troop.

The role of gunner/observer was an incredibly dangerous one in which a man not only had to cope with the enemy, but also had to place his life in the hands of a pilot, often an inexperienced one. Frederick Webb had been a patrol leader in the 1st Ramsgate (General Sir Charles Warren's Own) Troop, but in 1917, aged just 18, was serving as an Air Mechanic 2nd Class with the RFC in France. Like many such men, he also volunteered for flying duties as a gunner. Like 2nd Lieutenant Winser, above, he was serving with 43 Squadron but was killed in action on 29 July. From his burial place, which was home to a variety of

An FE2b similar to that in which 2nd Lieutenant Stevenson was killed. (Public Domain)

field hospitals during the war, it seems likely that Webb died of wounds sustained.[21]

One of the more prominent members of the organisation to lose his life around this time was Captain James Frederick Lorimer Fison, MC, who died at his home at Stutton Hall, Suffolk. Fison was a former head of school at Charterhouse and captain of the school's rifle corps, as well as being a prominent athlete. From Charterhouse he went on to study at Christ Church, Oxford, and became president of the common room as well as representing the college in both tennis and hockey. A deeply religious young man, Fison worked with the Charterhouse Mission at Southwark and with Pusey House in Oxford during his time at college and he became determined to dedicate his life to making a worthwhile contribution to British society. After leaving Oxford and returning to Suffolk, he threw himself into working with the Boy Scouts, rising to become the district commissioner for Ipswich. When war broke out Fison volunteered immediately and went on to serve with his battalion on the front lines, on the Divisional Headquarters Staff and as a Brigade Major. In June 1916 Fison was awarded the Military Cross for his courage in action and was also mentioned in despatches on two occasions. In March 1917 Captain Fison married Charlotte Patricia Hazel Elliot, the daughter of Lieutenant Colonel Elliot, DSO.[22] Captain Fison became the victim of a gas attack and was posted home due to his injuries; he contracted pneumonia and died on 2 November 1917 aged 27.

Of course, scouts served in the ranks as well as being officers and a great many were killed. Private Victor Bailey was a former member of the 1st Tyne Sea Scouts and had joined one of the many Pals' battalions formed across Britain. Having come through the devastation of the 20th (1st Tyneside Scottish) Northumberland Fusiliers on 1 July 1916 when it suffered 631 casualties, it would appear that Private Bailey survived the subsequent actions. On 5 June 1917 the Tyneside Scottish Brigade was preparing to assault Greenland Hill as part of the Arras offensive. The position was heavily defended but the brigade succeeded in taking its initial objective in the face of heavy losses. Private Victor Bailey was one of those to be killed during the attack. Like so many of the other ranks in the Tyneside Scottish there is relatively little known of Private Bailey's private life.[23]

It was not only the Western Front which was claiming victims, the fighting in Palestine continued to take a heavy toll Among these was Private Charles Ernest Albery, the former scoutmaster of 1st Salisbury Troop. By 1917 he was serving with 1/4 Wiltshire Regiment and was killed in action in Palestine aged 24 on 2 November 1917. Private Albery was from New Brompton in Kent and left behind a young widow. He is buried at Gaza War Cemetery.

We have already seen how keen some of the younger scouts were to get directly involved in the war effort, and September 1917 saw the loss of one of the youngest members of the scouts to be killed in action. Apprentice Frederick E. Temlett, from Neath Road in Plymouth, was a patrol leader with the 5th Plymouth Troop but had joined the Merchant Marine and was aged just 16 when he was killed. He was serving aboard the SS *Treverbyn*, a 4,163 ton steamer built by Redhead & Sons at South Shields in 1910, and part of the Hain SS Co. Ltd fleet out of St Ives.

On 3 September the *Treverbyn* was carrying a cargo of iron ore from Narvik to Manchester. When she was two miles off the Outer Hebrides she struck a mine laid by a U-Boat and was sunk. Twenty-seven men from the *Treverbyn* were lost, including Apprentice Temlett.[24]

We have already seen how a huge number of former scoutmasters joined up to answer the call to duty. Many of these went on to become commissioned officers but a great many served within the ranks. Arthur William Henry Curzon had been involved with the scout movement in Cambridge from its inception and had published a journal 'Fleur-de-lis' which explained the activities of local scouts. The journal included a note from Sir Robert Baden-Powell encouraging the local movement. Curzon went on to become the scoutmaster of the 1st Cambridge Sea Scouts after the Scout Troop disbanded in 1911. Mr Curzon had been an extremely popular and active scoutmaster and his troop was widely respected in Cambridge. Like so many who were involved in the movement, Mr Curzon had felt the pull of duty and had enlisted. On 8 July 1917 he was killed while serving as a Private in 1/1 Cambridgeshire Regiment. It would appear that the 34-year-old Private Curzon had died of wounds sustained in action as he is buried at Brandhoek Military Cemetery (the wartime home of several ambulance trains and a dressing station) in the West-Vlaanderen region of Belgium. Reflecting the high regard for Private Curzon, a memorial service was held for him at St Edward's Church on the morning of 19 August. The service was presided over by the Precentor of Trinity College, Captain J.H.C. How, and all members and former members of the local scouting movement were urged to attend.[25]

By the late summer, the fighting on the Western Front had reached such a devastating tempo that former scouts were dying in large numbers. Such was the rate of casualties that loved ones back home often only received the baldest of facts about the death of their beloved. Often these took the form of a short letter from the commanding officer of the man killed. Many of these letters, though well intentioned, followed a familiar pattern stating that the deceased had died instantly and felt no pain and that they had done their duty courageously. These letters often took a month or more to reach the grief-stricken in Britain but do seem to have provided some comfort. The parents of Private John Makin received such a letter at their home at 33 Foy Street, Wigan. In this case the letter came from Private Makin's platoon sergeant and perhaps reflected the fact that many officers had themselves become casualties. Private Makin had previously been a scout in one of the local troops and had worked with his father as a steeplejack. The sergeant informed Private Makin's parents that their son 'had died a true soldier's death, and was killed instantaneously', and said that he came from Leigh and was proud to be a country lad like their deceased son. Private Makin, 2 South Lancs, is commemorated on the Ypres (Menin Gate) Memorial.[26]

The East Ayrshire village of Mauchline also had its own scout troop. Before the war the assistant scoutmaster of the Mauchline Troop was a young scout named Archibald James Perry, the son of a Sergeant Major Perry and his wife, and was originally from Wiltshire. He had found employment in Mauchline as a footman to Sir Henry Farquhar at his Gilmilnscroft Estate. Archibald was described as an enthusiastic scout and had a history within the movement, having served as a scout and then as a patrol leader and King's Scout in the King's Athelston Troop, Malmesbury. When aged just 13 he had been presented with a merit medal by Sir Robert Baden-Powell after rescuing a boy from the River Avon. Unsurprisingly, Archibald decided to enlist in 1915, aged just 17. Initially he enlisted in the Royal Army Service Corps, but was then posted to the Warwick's before being sent to France. Upon arrival at the depot he was rebadged and joined the 1/7 Worcestershire Regiment; Archibald was killed in action on 16 August 1917. According to a letter from an army chaplain, Private Perry had initially been wounded in the leg and was being taken from the field of battle by a stretcher party when it too was hit. Private Perry was wounded again, in the stomach; he was taken to an Australian casualty clearing station at 2 am but died of his wounds just five hours later.

Mrs Mayer of Salt Heath, Stafford, had enjoyed a brief respite from worry at the end of August when her eldest son, Private Percy Arthur Frederick Moore, enjoyed a spell at home on leave. Private Moor was a former member of the Sandon Troop and had been employed at the shoe factory of Messrs Bostock; he enlisted in September 1914, aged 18, and joined 3 Coldstream Guards. By the time of his leave, he had been on the Western Front for two years and nine months; shortly after his return to the front he was killed. His captain wrote to his mother telling her that the company had been occupying the line when they came under very heavy shelling. The captain pointed out how courageous Private Moore and his comrades had been in standing up to the shelling, but that Private Moore and several others had been killed by an exploding shell. The letter concluded by informing the parents of Private Moore that his body had been buried on the battlefield.[27]

The chaos of the fighting on the Western Front could often mean that there was some confusion in assessing casualties and that families were often not notified of a loved one's fate for some time. In the case of one former scout it seems to have taken the authorities some eight

Private Moore.
(Staffordshire Advertiser)

months to notify the family that the young soldier was missing. Like so many former scouts, Private Herbert Liptrop had enlisted in November 1914, even though he was at the time aged just 17. To do so, he had left his employment as a flagger and slater in his hometown of Hindley, Wigan. Private Liptrop was killed on 31 July 1917 while serving with 18 Manchester. His family, however, do not seem to have been informed until March 1918 and even then they were only told that their son was missing. As a result, they placed desperate appeals for any information in the press.[28]

14 September saw the death of Berwick scout, Lance Corporal William Haswell Dickinson, who was killed while serving with 25 (Tyneside Irish) Northumberland Fusiliers, aged 22. Lance Corporal Dickinson was the son of James and Isabella Dickinson. His parents lived at Cramlington but had previously lived in Berwick, where Dickinson was born. He had been a member of the 1st Berwick Troop of the Northumberland Boy Scouts. Lance Corporal Dickinson died of wounds sustained while his battalion was occupying the lines near to Hargicourt. It would appear likely that he was evacuated

Private Herbert Liptrop. (Wigan Observer & District Advertiser)

from the lines and taken to the village of Tincourt which was a centre for casualty clearing stations but died of his wounds here.[29]

In October the parents of Sergeant Frederick John Jefferies received a telegram at their Trowbridge home telling them that their son had been killed. Sergeant Jefferies (21) was assistant scoutmaster in his hometown's troop and had been presented with a silver-mounted walking stick upon his promotion to this post. He was also well known as a solo singer at Westbury Parish Church. Joining up in September 1914, Jefferies had been posted to the Royal Engineers as a signaller. Mrs Jefferies received, along with the telegram, a letter detailing her son's death from his officer-in-command. Lieutenant Henry described how, on 20 September 1917, Sergeant Jefferies and several other men had been laying telegraph lines to trenches which had recently been captured. After coming under fire, the party got separated and Sergeant Jefferies made repeated attempts to gather them together again. While waiting for two members of the party to bring up fresh cabling, a heavy shell burst close to where Jefferies was standing and he was struck by a number of fragments. Sergeant Jefferies was immediately knocked unconscious and subsequently died without regaining consciousness.

The lieutenant went on to praise Sergeant Jefferies as the best man in his section, a friend, hard-working, conscientious and cheerful as well as being a good Christian man and a brave soldier. The lieutenant concluded by explaining how Sergeant Jefferies had been buried by two men who had been with him, and that another member of his section was fashioning a cross for the grave. Despite the promise to write once more when the cross had been fashioned, it seems that Sergeant Jefferies' hastily dug grave, like so many, was subsequently lost and he is commemorated at the Tyne Cot Memorial.

October also brought news of the death of Sergeant William Russell, another former scout from Berwick. Sergeant Russell was killed while serving with 1/7 Northumberland Fusiliers. Like so many of his fellow scouts from the area, he had joined the local Territorial battalion and was sent over to France in 1915 as a private. Once again, like so many former scouts, William proved himself an efficient soldier and, this being recognised, was promoted. It seems that news of his death took some time to filter home as his local newspaper included his name as being one of many who had donated sixpence to the local fund to aid in the purchase of cigarettes for soldiers. This list was published on 20 November, almost a month after Sergeant Russell's death on 26 October.[30]

While many former scouts who joined the RFC lost their lives either in training accidents or in combat over the skies of the Western Front, the RFC was also active in other theatres of war. The war in the Middle East was vastly different from that on the Western Front and diseases took a heavy toll of the men who served there. In 1917 the Germans had gained air superiority over the area and the army responded by forming 111 Squadron as the first allied fighter squadron in the area. After its formation in August, the squadron was equipped with Bristol F2b aircraft and flew missions to challenge the German fighters and to deny the enemy reconnaissance aircraft. Among the ranks of the squadron was 21-year-old Lieutenant Henry Joy McCracken. McCracken was a native of Belfast and had been a patrol leader in the 10th Belfast Troop. Sadly, he died of dysentery on 23 October.[31]

Lance Corporal Robert George Rowsell had been assistant scoutmaster of the Sowton Troop of Boy Scouts in East Devon and had joined the Devonshire Regiment in the summer of 1916 when still in his teens. He had first seen action on the occasion of his 20th birthday, in December 1916. By September 1917 Lance Corporal Rowsell was with the 9th battalion; his parents received the news that their only son had been wounded in the chest on 26 September and had succumbed to his injuries on 1 November. Subsequent reports highlighted how the young soldier had maintained a cheerful disposition and had made many friends among his comrades. Shortly after his death a letter arrived from the chaplain of the casualty clearing station detailing how their son had died. Unusually, the letter explained how Lance Corporal Rowsell had remained conscious until the moment of his death, but also sought to give reassurance by saying how the soldier had died like a brave lad.

On 2 November came the news of the death of 2nd Lieutenant Manfred Victor Johnstone Nash (36), former commissioner of scouts for the Alton district in Hampshire; Nash had been commissioned in the 1/10 London Regiment. By 1917 he was with his battalion in the Middle East and it was here, during the Third Battle of Gaza, that he was killed. 2nd Lieutenant Nash was the son of Ann Nash (his father, Frederick, was deceased) of 14 Eton Avenue, Hampstead, London, and had been educated (receiving an MA) at Exeter College, Oxford. Demonstrating his scouting ideals, his bereft mother had his headstone at Gaza War Cemetery inscribed with the following: 'HE STROVE TO HELP OTHERS TO HIGHER IDEALS OF DUTY AND SELF SACRIFICE.'

Lance Corporal Rowsell. (Exeter and Plymouth Gazette)

On the Western Front, November saw continued heavy losses. The nature of the fighting continued to cause confusion and the dates of death of several former scouts are difficult to establish. Typical of these instances is the death of Private Arthur Tugwell. Private Tugwell had formerly been a patrol leader in the Claygate Troop and had worked at an ironmongers. Like so many, he had answered his country's call and had enlisted in the East Surrey. By November he had been posted to the 76th Company, Machine Gun Corps. It is known that the 20-year-old soldier was killed at some point in November, but the exact date is a mystery. The Commonwealth War Graves Commission lists his death as having occurred on 29 November, but his parents appear to have been informed far earlier with a death notification appearing in the *Surrey Advertiser* on 12 November.[32]

December brought news of the severe wounding of another scout. Private K.G. Kinghorn (20) was patrol leader of the 3rd Elswick (14th Newcastle) Troop and had been involved with the organisation for several years. Originally from the border village of Norham, Private Kinghorn had left for Newcastle with his widowed mother and found work with the North Eastern Railway as a mineral clerk at Percy Main. Determined to do his bit for King and country, Kinghorn tried to enlist immediately war had been declared but was denied for several months due to his employment on the railways. When he did eventually get permission, his colleagues made a gift of a silver cigarette case to him. The scout leader had initially joined the Northumberland Fusiliers but had been attached to the Royal Fusiliers (London Regiment) when he was sent to the front. In December, the young soldier was badly wounded in the face and evacuated to a military hospital at Colchester. According to a letter received shortly before Christmas Private Kinghorn had been gravely wounded and had lost his right eye, but was making satisfactory progress. Thankfully, it seems that Private Kinghorn survived his injuries.

On 30 December, 2nd Lieutenant Harold Walter Barnett was killed in action. The 22-year-old subaltern was serving with 5 South Lancs and before the war had been assistant scoutmaster of St John's Troop. He was a native of Deptford, London, where his parents lived at 64 Ashmead Road.[33]

CHAPTER 5

1918

Home Front

The impression held by some that the Boy Scouts were a quasi-military organisation continued throughout the war, despite the best attempts of the movement to provide reassurance. Some of the duties undertaken by the scouts did indeed lay them open to such accusations. Certainly, there were those who viewed the scouts as being a form of embryonic soldiers or sailors who were being trained specifically for future service in the armed forces. The association denied this and insisted that the scouts were merely being trained to be good citizens. In the face of these suspicions the press did its best to reassure readers by highlighting the good character of the individual scouts and by praising the work they were doing for their country.

The Times History and Encyclopedia of the War agreed with the rest of the press regarding the non-military aspect of the movement when it summed up the contributions of the Boy Scouts Association in a 1918 issue. It stated that of over 100 different badges and awards which a scout could attain, before 1914 there was only one, marksmanship, which was even slightly military. Other examples quoted included farming, leatherworking, gardener, handyman and interpreter. Furthermore, the essential outcome of scout training was not a form of military discipline but that of self-governance and self-discipline.

Among the scouts themselves, one of the most coveted of wartime honours was to be awarded the War Service Badge. The badge was very difficult to obtain as a scout had to undertake service to the country for twenty-eight days (later fifty) of unpaid work. During the course of the war some 80,000 of these badges were awarded, demonstrating the commitment of the scouts to the national effort. Alongside the prestigious War Service Badge were three more awards: the Certificate of Merit, the Medal of Merit and the Silver Wolf. The last of these was only awardable at the discretion of the Chief Scout himself and was awarded to King's Scouts or King's Sea Scouts who had earned twelve proficiency badges and had at least two years' service and who had performed in exceptional circumstances such as saving a life or carrying out repeated acts of bravery, endurance or self-sacrifice. The highest award possible for a scout was the Cross for Gallantry in Saving Life, which was separated into three grades. In descending order they were: the bronze cross (worn on a red ribbon) for special heroism, the silver cross (worn on a blue ribbon) was for gallantry with considerable risk, while the gilt cross (worn on a blue ribbon with red stripes) was awarded for exceptional action in an emergency without risk.[1]

Although the collection of money from the public was technically against the principles of the scouts, the boys themselves raised funds extensively. Many of the funds raised were on behalf of the Cornwell Memorial Fund (in honour of boy sailor VC and boy scout Jack Cornwell) and by 1918 boy scouts had contributed some £1,487 to the fund.

The Sea Scouts also made a huge contribution to the war effort. We have already seen how they mounted guard over Britain's coasts. Throughout the war a very efficient force of 1,400 sea scouts were serving in this capacity. They were under the command of veteran members of the coastguard and Petty Officers of the Royal Navy. This was an arduous duty and the boys received pay in lieu of rations for serving in this capacity. The pay rate was 18s a week and the boys performed their own catering, cooking and looking after their quarters. Their coast-watching duties consisted of keeping guard, signalling, telephoning and acting as dispatch-riders on their bicycles.

The sea scouts mounting coastal patrols performed admirably and the role they played was an incredibly valuable one. Typical of the log-books that were maintained by the sea scouts was one quoted in *The Times History and Encyclopedia of the War* which read: 'Warned a destroyer off the rocks in fog; Sighted and reported airship going S.S.E. five miles distant; Provided night guard over damaged seaplane, which was towed ashore by drifter … Floating mine reported by fishing boat – Proceeded with the patrol boat which located and blew up the mine'.[2]

The sea scouts did not, however, limit themselves to coastal watches. Following the scout law of doing a good turn for someone every day they, in their off-duty hours, helped the local fishermen and farmers. This willingness to pitch in won them almost universal praise from the communities in which they were based.

The scouts and sea scouts came from a variety of backgrounds but many, it cannot be denied, were from better-off, middle-class backgrounds and the organisation, along with those such as the Boys' Brigade, was often looked on askance by boys of the lower classes. Indeed, throughout the war there were small-scale incidents of scouts being abused by working-class boys.

The background of some of the wealthier scouts meant that the hardships which they endured in some of their duties, notably those of the sea scouts employed on coastguard duties, were completely foreign to them. Patrolling a cold, wet, windy coastline in the pitch dark without adequate clothing or equipment was a trying experience to say the least, but the vast majority undertook their duties without complaint, and even enthusiastically. Many scoutmasters put this down to the indescribable concept of 'pluck' which was encouraged in the scouting movement.

The abilities of the sea scouts sometimes surprised the coastguards with whom they were stationed. In one case a coastguard station had lost five of its six-man complement (drafted into Royal Navy). The Petty Officer left in command had been told to expect a party of sea scouts to take the place of the missing men and had laid in a supply of meat which he deemed sufficient for the five boys for a single day, but he was at a loss as to how it was to be cooked. When the scouts arrived, they quickly assessed the situation. The leader of the sea scouts assured the Petty Officer that the supply was sufficient for two-and-a-half days, and that the sea scout cook would immediately cook today's supply. The sea scouts placed two of their number on watch and the others formed their camp. The Petty Officer was very pleasantly surprised and favourably compared the abilities of the scouts with the men whom they had replaced.

Such ability was put down largely to the spirit which had been engendered in the Sea Scouts (and Scouts) and this was further reinforced by the number of reports throughout the war (but especially in the first two years of the war) of sea scouts on coastguard duties who were due leave over the Christmas period, voluntarily giving up the pleasures of a family Christmas in favour of their duties (this was put down to a suspicion among the boys that the Germans would use the holiday to launch an attack).

Although the activities and usefulness of scouts and former scouts to the military cannot be overestimated, it was in its contribution on the Home Front that the movement made its most active and valuable contributions. In national and local government the scouts made an unobtrusive but very valuable contribution to the working of government departments in a wide variety of ways. One British General even remarked that, whenever he entered a new place, he always looked for a Boy Scout to act as guide. By this stage of the war the scouts had proven themselves so effective in this capacity that many adult citizens would have echoed the General.

For many scouts and former scouts who were still underage for the services there was, despite growing awareness of the horrors of the Western Front, a keenness to actively contribute to the war effort. Many gained employment in the munitions industry and felt that this was the next best thing to enlisting.

In May one of these boys found himself at the centre of the local media spotlight. Kenneth Puttock (16) from Weybridge was working as a turner's improver at the firm of Gordon Watney & Co. Kenneth was a former scout who was a good all-round sportsman. A keen footballer (he had played outside left for St James' School team in 1915–16) and a good swimmer, he also held the junior championship of the Weymouth Rifle Club and had won the Lord Robert's medal, the Donegall badge, a *Daily Telegraph* certificate and a club badge for qualifying on the service rifle at Bisley.

On Sunday 19 May he was taking advantage of a day off to go canoeing on the River Wey with his sister. The two had just pulled into the bankside opposite Overmead so that they could swap seats. While they were doing so, they saw another canoe capsize in deep water. The canoe held two wounded soldiers from a nearby military hospital. Seeing that the soldiers were in difficulties, Kenneth immediately took off his jacket and entered the water to render assistance. He got hold of one soldier and held him up until a punt containing three ladies pulled the soldier aboard. The other soldier had gone under the water for the last time and Kenneth immediately dived down to the bottom and managed to bring him to the surface.

The two exhausted soldiers, neither of whom could swim and one of whom was lame, were cared for at the home of Mr H.V. Lancaster, Overmead, before being sent back to the military hospital. Kenneth was looked after and given a change of clothing by M B. Wilkinson of Sandy Banks before being sent home.

As a former scout who had absorbed the lessons of humility, Kenneth did not mention the deed to any of his friends or family. The soldiers, however, freely admitted that they owed their lives to young Kenneth and on Saturday 25 May an anonymous letter arrived at the premises of Watney & Co. The firm was having an entertainment programme in the works' canteen theatre that evening and Major Gordon Watney and the other directors took advantage of this to tell the workers of Kenneth's actions and to present him with a silver watch and chain.

We have already seen how the scouts made a massive contribution to agriculture. In addition to the flax harvest, other crops also gave work to the scouts. In 1918 some 500 London scouts, for example, found employment in the fields around Dorset, Lincolnshire, Middlesex and Norfolk. The severe labour shortage which was affecting many parts of rural Britain at this time ensured that the use of the boy scouts found favour both in central government and in most local authorities.

The use of the boy scouts to aid with the harvest was not without its critics, however. Some worried that the use of school-age scouts during term time would adversely affect their education. At Guildford, the topic of using boy scouts to help gather the harvest resulted in a spirited debate in the council during the final year of the war. The County Commissioner of Boy Scouts, General Sir Edmond Elles, had requested that scouts aged between 12 and 14 be released from school so that they could help in fruit picking and haymaking in June, the corn harvest and hops in August, and in potato lifting and haymaking in September and October. The Education Commission had agreed to this request as the boys would be certified as working on the land and would be under the guidance of a scoutmaster. One councillor, Mr A. Edwards, argued that if this was to be allowed for scouts then it should be acceptable for any boy to volunteer, but was informed that this was not possible and that the scouts were going as part of an approved and recognised organisation. It was also argued that it might serve as an inducement for other boys to join the scouts.

Another councillor, Mrs Harris, argued that she could not see how a boy aged 14 who obtained a job in agriculture could be refused if the scouts were allowed to go, but had concerns that boys were being removed from schooling at the most important point in their education. She also had concerns over how the scoutmasters would be able to keep an eye on their charges when they were dispersed over a wide area and asked if the opinions of local headmasters should not be sought. Councillor Mr J.A. Christopher argued that with many allotment holders having been called up, the scouts should be put to work on allotments too.

The chair of the committee stated that the boys would not lose much schooling as part of the harvest occurred during the summer break in any case, and that he was surprised there should be opposition to Guildford scouts doing what other scouts were doing all over the country; he further said that the presence of a scoutmaster on a permanent basis was irrelevant as the scouts would be supervised at all times. Mrs Harris and Mr Edwards then moved that the matter be put back before the Education Committee and that the views of headmasters should be sought before any decision was made.

The Mayor spoke in opposition to this, saying that it was a case of accepting a 'lesser evil'. The question was a simple one: 'Were the crops to be saved or allowed to spoil?'[3] Mr Hughes supported the Mayor and the committee from a patriotic view and stated that with the shortage of labour some 12,000 scouts had been asked for, and the question of gathering in the harvest was a particularly problematic one that year. The vote was then held, and the amendment was defeated.

One of the more unusual collections that was undertaken by the scouts was that of plum stones. The movement organised itself across the country to undertake the collection of the stones as they were used to produce charcoal which was used in the anti-gas respirators of the British Army. It had been found that the charcoal from the plum stones was far more absorbent than that produced from other sources and so they were highly prized by the authorities. Once again, the organisation of the Boy Scouts Association meant that it was ideally suited to the task.

Although the Boy Scout movement continued to remain popular throughout the war, there were some areas in which wartime demands had resulted in a negative impact on the movement. In Newcastle-under-Lyme, Staffordshire, for example, membership in the organisation had fallen off severely by the summer of 1918. In September, a decision was made to try to reverse this slump and on 10 September a series of meetings was held in the town. Present at the meetings were the Earl of Dartmouth (Lord Lieutenant and the President of the Boy Scouts in the county), Mr Twyford (the President for Newcastle-under-Lyme), Ronald Copeland (Commissioner for the Newcastle-under-Lyme district), and, representing Sir Robert Baden-Powell, Mr Elwes. Mr Elwes gave a speech which illustrated the activities of the Boy Scouts during both peace and war, and gave a description of the marked good effect that membership had on a boy's character.

These meetings were part of a wider movement across the Potteries. The previous weekend had seen a large-scale inspection parade overseen by Lady Joan Legge and Colonel Ulrick de Burgh at Stoke while the same couple inaugurated a new branch of the association at Leek on the same day as the meetings at Newcastle-under-Lyme.

By this stage of the war, and with many people becoming increasingly concerned about the militarisation of society and the scale of youthful losses in the war, there was a growing sense that those attempting to publicise the movement were anxious to refute, or at least to lessen, the militaristic side of scouting. Thus, the article 'The Boy Scout Movement', in the *Staffordshire Sentinel* on 11 September, which described the above meetings and parades, also had a long passage describing how the movement was not primarily militaristic, saying that 'Boy Scouts are not, and are not intended to be, a military organisation,' before adding, 'though a Boy Scout is wishful to do whatever duty falls to his lot.' Rather, the emphasis was placed upon the useful and necessary training which was undertaken for 'their physical, moral and spiritual well-being, so that they may grow up into self-respecting and respected citizens'.[4] In an effort to boost popularity, the article also stated that being a scout represented the chance of having fun too.

By the end of the war the numerous recreation huts at the front, funded by the efforts of boy scouts such as those in Belfast, had more than proven their worth. A visitors' book in one such hut contained the signatures of more than 4,000 old scouts who had been soldiers at the front.

Another official tribute which came the way of the Boy Scouts toward the end of the war was a letter of thanks from the Secretary of War which praised the Boy Scouts Association for the work which it had performed in the recruiting campaign.

Military Service

The first day of January also brought news of the return of a former Berwick scout to his home. Robert Cooper Clements, the Berwick District Secretary for the Boy Scouts Association and scoutmaster of the Spittal Troop, had gone to France with the Northumberland Fusiliers and had been promoted to the rank of Regimental Quartermaster Sergeant by 1916, he was then further promoted to Sergeant Major. With the carnage of 1916 and 1917 the British Army was running short of suitable officer candidates and many Non-commissioned Officers (NCOs) were offered the chance of a commission. Clements had been one such NCO and by January he was an officer cadet and was given a period of leave, during which he returned to his home (he also had a brother who was serving as a Captain in the Northumberland Fusiliers). He had returned to Britain upon being offered the chance to train for a commission and was looking forward to becoming an officer, like his brother.

Those scouts and former scouts who joined the army soon proved their worth with many going on to earn decorations, while others provided a good reinforcement for the officer corps. The army, too, quickly learned that ex-scouts usually made for very efficient soldiers. They adapted to army life quickly and the techniques that they had learned in the scouts proved very useful during army life. Former scouts wrote back home telling friends and relatives how they had found that even small things learned in the scouts, such as how to fold their blankets, were proving useful and that other men were learning from them. One former scout wrote home shortly after joining the army to say how the men of his section were already referring to him, unofficially, as corporal because his knowledge had proven so useful to them.

Such factors resulted in many scouts quickly being promoted to the rank of NCO due to the skills and leadership qualities which they had developed in the Boy Scouts. One scoutmaster wrote to his association telling them that every one of his boys who had joined up had immediately been made NCOs. Another former scout, himself a lance corporal, wrote how he had quickly discovered that any former scout joining his battalion had no difficulty in being made up to the rank. An experienced lieutenant, himself a former scoutmaster, writing home of the scouts in his command said that they were, 'Grand chaps all of them … it certainly makes all the difference to me to have some Scouts in the ranks.'[5] In a similar vein another officer wrote of how the five former scouts in his command were better soldiers when they arrived than other volunteers would ever be. Another wrote of the dozen scouts in his battalion, describing how five were NCOs, four were in the battalion scout section, one was in transport and the remaining two were trained as signallers. Clearly the presence of these skills made a great difference to front-line officers and greatly improved efficiency. It was not only the skills of the scouts that made them so appreciated, however. The ability of former scouts to pass on their knowledge to their fellow soldiers was also greatly appreciated by officers. One army chaplain wrote of this, saying that their 'influence upon other fellows was splendid'.

The German offensive which began on 25 March 1918, throwing a large portion of the British Army back in utter confusion, was a time of great sacrifice and hardship. Among the officers fighting in this area at the time was Captain Alfred Maurice Toye of 2 Middlesex (Duke of Cambridge's Own) Regiment. Toye had been brought up in an atmosphere of duty, loyalty and the ethos of the British Army. He was born at Aldershot in 1897 with his father, James Robert Toye, being an army pensioner and clerk. Unsurprisingly, Toye joined the Boy Scouts and became a patrol leader in the 2nd Aldershot Troop. On 25 March 1918 he found himself and his men being overrun by the enemy attack on Eterpigny Ridge. Three times he re-established a post which had been overrun, and when three neighbouring posts were cut off he fought his way back to British lines with just one other officer and six other ranks. He immediately gathered seventy men and led a counter-attack before taking up a line which he defended until reinforcements arrived on the scene. In two operations following this he oversaw the covering of his battalion as it retired before the enemy advance. During this time he was wounded twice but remained at his post. For his actions, the former scout was awarded the VC which was presented to him by the King at Aldershot in June. Just a week after his investiture Captain Toye, VC, MC, was married to his sweetheart, Flora, née Robertson.[6]

On 25 April Lance Corporal Thomas Augustus Paris (21) of 25 London (Cyclists) Regiment was killed in action while serving on attachment to the 2/10 London's. This was the period of the Germans' Spring Offensive when British lines were being overrun and there were very heavy casualties. The chaotic nature of the fighting saw many men fighting in ad-hoc and hastily formed units in an effort to plug the ruptured lines. As a result the records of casualties were somewhat chaotic and the usual system, which was far from perfect, badly disrupted. Thus, it is impossible to say exactly where Lance Corporal Paris was killed and, like many lost during this time, his remains were not recovered and he is commemorated on the Pozieres Memorial.

Captain Toye being presented with his VC by the King. (Hampshire and Solent Museums, CC.2.0)

Lance Corporal Paris was from Ilford, where he lived with his father at 582 Green Lane, Goodmayes, and had been the assistant scoutmaster of 1 Chadwell Heath Troop.[7]

The war took a terrible toll on members of the scouts, but death did not always come at the front. Private Walter Ingham had been a member of the St Peter's Troop. A native of Burnley, where he had worked on the trams, Walter had joined up, enlisting in Scottish Rifles in June 1915. He had been out in France on two occasions and had been badly wounded to the extent that he was declared unfit for military service abroad and transferred to the RAMC and posted to the General Northern Hospital at Newcastle upon Tyne. It was here that he developed bronchitis which turned into pneumonia. Private Walter Ingham was aged just 22 when he died on 19 May. His body was brought back, at his request, to Burnley for burial (despite the fact that he had been offered a full military funeral at Newcastle).

Just one day after the death of Private Ingham the battle on the Western Front claimed the life of another former scout. Private John Smith Davidson Baigrie of 18 Highland Light Infantry was killed, aged just 18. A native of Newbattle, Lothian, he was the youngest

Private Walter Ingham.
(Burnley Express and Advertiser)

son in the family and had moved with his father to Heatherie Hall, West Linton, Peeblesshire. Prior to joining up he had been the deputy assistant scoutmaster to 8 Midlothian Troop. Private Baigrie is buried at Martinsart British Cemetery. For the Baigrie family this was the second son to be lost in the war. Private William Baigrie of 15 Highland Light Infantry had been killed, aged 27, on 30 November 1917 and is commemorated at Tyne Cot.

The summer of 1918 saw a steady number of casualties as the Allies prepared to advance. Private Samuel George Eley, from

Epsom, had been assistant scoutmaster with 1 Epsom Troop and a keen member of the Epsom Rifle Club. Like many scouts he found himself on the front lines and was serving with 9 Machine Gun Corps when he lost his life on 19 July aged just 20.[8]

We have seen many times just how eager many young scouts were to enlist and get into the action at the front. Many joined up before they were 18. One of these was Sapper William Mills of Horsell, Woking. William joined up when he was aged just 16 and appears to have been sent to the front when still just 17. He had served with the Royal Engineers on the Western Front for two years. In the final weeks of the war he was part of the 141st Army Troops Company, RE. In late September 1918 his parents received the dreaded news that their 19-year-old son had been killed. Sapper Mills had been standing near a house with two comrades when there was an explosion and he was struck on the head and killed instantly by a piece of masonry. Before the war, in addition to being a scout, Mills had been a pupil at Horsell School and a carpentry apprentice in his hometown. This courageous and determined young man had been wounded twice during his service at the front.[9]

At least twenty-one former scouts were awarded the VC during the war, the last, to Private Robert Edward Cruickshank, was announced in October 1918. Although Private Cruickshank's father had been born in Aberdeen, Private Cruickshank himself had been born at Winnipeg in Canada before his family moved back to Britain when he was aged just 3. Private Cruickshank had been an assistant scoutmaster in the 53rd North London Troop. After leaving school he had become a travelling salesman for the Lever Company. Robert had a keen interest in both military matters and politics (in addition to the scouting movement) and joined The City of London Yeomanry (Rough Riders) and spoke in support of his local MP on several occasions. In 1915, aged 27, Cruickshank had enlisted in the RFC but in November of that year he transferred to the London Regiment. In September 1916 he was wounded twice, the final time on the Somme at Leuze Wood. His injuries were so severe that he was evacuated home and spent the next few months recuperating in Britain. In January 1917 he was posted to 2/14 London Regiment (London Scottish) and joined them at Salonika, preparatory to going to Egypt. Robert was the eldest of three brothers, all of whom were former scouts. One of his brothers, Percy C.W. Cruickshank was killed on 22 January 1917 while serving as a private in 4 London Regiment.[10]

On 1 May 1918 his battalion was engaged in a heavy action with Turkish troops on the banks of the Jordan River. Robert's platoon came under heavy fire and was forced to take cover in a wadi, but most were hit before they reached the bottom. The commanding officer was shot and killed; the sergeant who took over sent a runner back to ask for support, but was also shot dead almost immediately thereafter. The only remaining NCO was a lance corporal and, believing the first messenger must have been killed, asked for volunteers. Robert stepped forward. He rushed up the slope but was immediately hit and rolled back down to the bottom of the wadi. Robert made another attempt but was again hit. After having his wounds dressed he made a third attempt but was hit again. He was now so badly wounded that he was unable to stand and so he rolled himself back down the slope amid a hail of sniper shots. Robert was now unable to carry on and lay where he fell under fire for the rest of the day. During this time he was once again wounded but remained uncomplaining. As a result of his injuries Robert was shipped back to Britain and was fêted as a hero when his courageous actions were brought to the attention of the public. On 24 October Robert, accompanied by his mother and his fiancée, attended Buckingham Palace for his investiture.[11]

As the British Army advanced into the final months of the war, a great many men who had served throughout lost their lives now the end of the conflict was in sight. We have already seen how the secretary of the Boy Scout movement in Berwick, Robert Cooper Clements, had gone to France in 1915 with the Northumberland Fusiliers and that by the beginning of January 1918 he was studying for his commission. Clements successfully obtained his commission and was sent back to the front as a 2nd Lieutenant. On 8 August the men of 4 Northumberland Fusiliers were preparing to advance upon Lille and 2nd Lieutenant

Clements (35) was sent forward to make a reconnaissance. During this scouting mission the brave officer was killed in action. Like so many others, the grief of 2nd Lieutenant Clements' family was made worse by initial confusion over his fate; 2nd Lieutenant Clements was initially posted missing but at the end of August his family received notification that he was a prisoner of war. Later it was confirmed that this was not the case, but that the fate of Lieutenant Clements remained a mystery. It would appear that he was initially buried at Outterstene Communal Cemetery Extension, but under a cross which identified him as a 2nd Lieutenant R.C. Clements of 8 Royal Irish Fusiliers. An exhumation took place on 11 March 1921, during which identification was confirmed.

Private Robert Cruickshank VC, seen here in 1915. (Public Domain)

Lieutenant Clements was identified by his remains (he was apparently only 5ft 3in and had several false teeth, which were recovered) and by the presence of regimental buttons from the Northumberland Fusiliers. Lieutenant Clements left behind his parents and his widow, Minnie (who lived at 1 Wilson's Terrace, Spittal).

The start of September 1918 brought the news of the death in action of one of the most decorated NCO former scouts. Sergeant Arthur Wesley Chambers (30) was killed on 2 September while serving at the front with the 11th Division Signal Company, Royal Engineers. Sergeant Chambers was killed during the Battle of the Drocourt-Queant Line. Before the war

Sergeant Chambers had been a pioneer in the scouting movement in the district of Slough. He had gone on to become the first district scoutmaster of the Slough Boy Scout Association and had also been the captain of the 1st Slough Company of the Boys' Life Brigade and, for many years, had been a member of the choir of the Wesleyan Chapel at Herschel Street in Slough. Sergeant Chambers had proven to be a very courageous soldier and had earned the Military Medal and bar and had recently been recommended for the Distinguished Conduct Medal (DCM) but this was downgraded to a Meritorious Service Medal (MSM).[12]

September also brought slightly better, though still worrying, news to the Ormskirk family of 2nd Lieutenant T.J.E. Barclay, Royal Scots. A telegram arrived informing them that their son had been wounded in the left shoulder on 1 September and was in hospital at Winnercux. 2nd Lieutenant Barclay was one of those who had benefited greatly from his time in the Ormskirk Scouts Defence Corps before he had joined the army. This was the second time that the lieutenant had been wounded for he had been injured in the right hand on 27 July, but on that occasion had decided to remain with his unit.[13]

The final 100 days of the war saw the British Army advancing rapidly and the largely static trench warfare of the previous years gave way to warfare in open countryside in many places. Despite the fact that it was obvious that the allies were going to win the war, the remaining German army units put up a spirited defence and casualties among the advancing forces were high. Among them was yet another Berwick scout. Lance Corporal Joseph Weatherly was killed while serving with 9 (Northumberland Hussars) Northumberland Fusiliers on 24 October, just eighteen days before the armistice.[14]

Two days after the armistice was declared on 11 November, another former scout lost his life. 22-year-old Corporal Frederick Stanley Spurin, MM, of 4 King's Royal Rifle Corps had formerly been assistant scoutmaster of 110 North London Troop and was from Finsbury Park Road.[15] His father had the following inscription placed upon his headstone: 'A LOYAL SCOUT HE WAS PREPARED.'

Conclusion

By the end of the war the Boy Scout Association could be rightly proud of its wartime contributions both on the Home Front and on the various war fronts. Tens of thousands of scouts and former scouts had volunteered, and many had been killed, but these were only the tip of the iceberg when it came to the movement's contribution.

On the Home Front the scouts had participated in a great variety of useful activities. These included the initial efforts at providing guards at vulnerable points, helping with the harvest and with other agricultural tasks, providing useful services to governmental offices, both national and local, and fundraising through useful activities such as collecting used bottles and waste paper. The scouts also aided in the purchasing of recreational huts and ambulances for the front and these efforts, which often went largely unrecognised, were appreciated by the troops, even if they were largely unaware of the source of them.

Attitudes towards the movement varied considerably. Many in authority welcomed the contribution and ethos of the Boy Scouts and equally, many civilians were also grateful and recognised the contributions made by the boys. Others were ambivalent, suspicious, or even openly hostile towards the association and towards the boys themselves. Those who were suspicious of authority were automatically suspicious of an organisation which fostered an ethos of absolute obedience to one's superiors. The greatest hostility towards boy scouts was usually found in the cities and large industrial towns. The scouting movement was seen as elitist and many boys simply could not afford to join even if they had wanted to. In such places the vast majority of boys were expected to find work to help to support themselves and their families as soon as they left school at the age of 14. To join the scouts for these boys was simply impossible. It would mark one out as a shirker, preferring to play at soldiers than to find work. Part of this attitude was the importance attached to work in the role of working-class men at the time. With little to look forward to and little chance of financial or social betterment, working-class male society tended to define itself using a form of hyper-masculinity in which manual labour played a huge role. Boys brought up in this atmosphere looked askance at the Boy Scouts, with their uniforms, badges and conformity to the rules. Often these attitudes turned towards active hostility and there were many occasions of Boy Scout parades or other activities being disrupted by hostile gangs of boys who would jeer at, or even physically confront the scouts, either by assaulting them or by throwing stones. Although the scouts attempted to improve their record in recruiting these 'bad boys', the record in this respect remained largely poor throughout the war.

There were, however, some criticisms of the movement, as we have seen. The most vociferous criticism came from those who accused the association of encouraging militarism. Although the association had made strenuous attempts to discredit and refute such criticism, there was undoubtedly some truth in it. Although the scouts were conceived of in peacetime as an organisation which would take young boys and teach them useful skills and shape their character to ensure that they became useful citizens, the war did bring about a subtle shift in character. Many of the wartime activities did indeed have a military bent. Marksmanship and musketry tests became far more prevalent, as did other scout skills which had military applications. Many outdoor activities also took on a more militaristic tone, such as the wargames that took place in many places.

Although many of the badges which were earned by the scouts during the war maintained the peacetime traditions of scouting, it cannot be denied that those with a military use became more popular as a result of the war. The fact that scouts had been brought up to believe in obeying the orders of their superiors without question (albeit alongside the encouragement of initiative too) and in an ethos of loyalty and duty to King and country meant that the older scouts were ready-made material for the forces, while the younger boys, in the febrile wartime atmosphere, were being strongly inculcated with the desire to join the forces as soon as they were able to do so.

Many of the upper echelons of the scouts' officer corps were former military men. The ranks of the district commissioners and so on were dominated by former military officers. The organisational scheme of the association added to the military theme. The uniform, the fact that medals were awarded for demonstrations of courage and bravery, the belief that orders from superiors should be obeyed without question, all of these were quasi-military trappings and it is clear and undeniable that the Boy Scouts Association did indeed have a strong military leaning.

It is equally clear from studying the exercises in which scouts took part during their summer camps or other outdoor events that the war had indeed caused an increasing militarisation in the association. This was only natural. By mid-1915 it was becoming increasingly apparent that this war was different to those that had gone before, and not what had been expected by those cheering crowds who welcomed the outbreak of war. To those who could read the signs it seemed that the war was going to last far longer than had been expected, and that many more young men would be required to join the colours. Those who had been boy scouts, as we have repeatedly seen, tended to make dedicated and able soldiers and it was only natural that the association would seek to increase the levels of training that might come in handy in military service. Another driving factor behind the increasing militarism of the movement was the boys themselves. During the first three years of the war there was a glamour about the soldiery that could commonly be seen on the streets of Britain (indeed, this glamour persisted among some on the Home Front, although the catastrophes of 1916 and the attrition of 1917 lessened enthusiasm considerably) and it was to be expected that boys, especially those who were members of the Boy Scouts, would wish to emulate their heroes.

The question of the increasing militarism of the movement as a result of the war was one which hung over the association throughout the war but especially after the formation of the Scouts Defence Corps. The greatest contribution of the corps to the war effort was surely in the basic infantry training that it gave to members before many of them either enlisted or, increasingly, were conscripted into the army. The corps was overall, however, a failure; numbers, while on the face of it impressive, never reached the levels expected in many areas and the main purpose of the force was undermined as invasion became less and less likely and conscription into the forces replaced voluntarism, meaning that a larger force of soldiers was available in Britain.

As we have seen, despite the denials, the movement had indeed become more militarised by the war. In many ways the war had given the movement an extra layer of definition and purpose. After all, scouts were brought up to acknowledge their duty to King and country, and wartime service was the ultimate expression of this duty. The question at the end of the war was: how would the association develop when once more faced with peacetime, and a peacetime which lay in the shadow of the great carnage of the First World War and an increasing belief in pacifism?

Endnotes

Chapter 1: 1914

1. *Hampshire Independent*, 15 August 1914, p. 4.
2. *Berks and Oxon Advertiser*, 28 August 1914, p. 6.
3. *Hastings & St Leonards Observer*, 15 August 1914, p. 4.
4. *Birmingham Daily Post*, 14 August 1914, p. 6.
5. *Derbyshire Courier*, 15 August 1914, p. 5.
6. *Hampshire Independent*, 15 August 1914, p. 4.
7. *Illustrated London News*, 22 August 1914, p. 4.
8. *Daily Mirror*, 13 August 1914, p. 3.
9. *Jarrow Express*, 18 December 1914, p. 11.
10. Ibid.
11. *Alderley & Wilmslow Advertiser*, 11 December 1914, p. 8.
12. *Hampshire Telegraph*, 18 December 1914, p. 13.
13. Captain Gordon-Duff is buried at Rue-Du-Bois Military Cemetery, Fleurbaix.
14. Private Walker is buried at Bethune Town Cemetery.
15. Sergeant White is buried at Bethune Town Cemetery.
16. *Dublin Daily Express,* 19 December 1914, p. 1. Lance Corporal Daphne is buried at Lancashire Cottage Cemetery.
17. Captain Sir Montague A.R. Cholmeley is commemorated on the Le Touret Memorial.
18. Private Caulder is buried at Bethune Town Cemetery.

Chapter 2: 1915

1. *Western Gazette*, 1 January 1915, p. 8.
2. *Yorkshire Evening Post*, 16 January 1915, p. 6.

3. *Aberdeen Evening News*, 28 January 1915, p. 4.

4. *Rugby Advertiser*, 30 January 1915, p. 6.

5. The world was shocked by the events in Louvain. Not only by the massacre of civilians but also the burning of the medieval cathedral with its vast and priceless library. An estimated 230,000 volumes were lost in the destruction, including Gothic and Renaissance manuscripts and a collection of over 1,750 medieval manuscripts and books.

6. *Rugby Advertiser*, 13 February 1915, p. 5.

7. *Sheffield Daily Telegraph*, 16 February 1915, p. 5.

8. A comparison could be made between the Scouts Defence Corps and the LDV/Home Guard in the Second World War. Clearly, both were military forces.

9. *Bath Chronicle and Weekly Gazette*, 1 May 1915, p. 6.

10. *Dublin Daily Express*, 30 June 1915, p. 3.

11. *The Kingston Times*, 21 August 1915, p. 6.

12. *Newcastle Journal*, 29 October 1915, p. 6.

13. Corporal Garrod is buried at Lowestoft (Normanston Drive) Cemetery.

14. Private Ireland is commemorated on the Le Touret Memorial.

15. Private Dutton is buried at Bois-Grenier Communal Cemetery.

16. Lieutenant West's body was not recovered and he is commemorated on the Ypres (Menin Gate) Memorial.

17. Lance Corporal Thompson is buried at Twelve Tree Copse Cemetery.

18. Private Hendry is commemorated on the Helles Memorial.

19. Corporal Sumption is commemorated on the Helles Memorial.

20. 2nd Lieutenant Meldrum is commemorated on the Neuve-Chapelle Memorial.

21. 2nd Lieutenant Hare is commemorated on the Loos Memorial.

22. *Morpeth Herald*, 15 January 1915, p. 9.

23. Both Surgeon Hibbert and Private Tungate are commemorated on the Chatham Naval Memorial.

24. Boy 1st Class Gasson is commemorated on the Portsmouth Naval Memorial.

25. Corporal Pond appears to have survived the war. The Essex Yeomanry served with the 8th Cavalry Bgd, 3rd Cavalry Division, and had a relatively quiet war. Its next participation in a major battle came in 1917 when it fought on the opening day of the Battle of Arras. It then suffered significant losses during the German offensive of March 1918 and was broken up with A Squadron being sent to the 5th, B Company became part of the 2nd Dragoon Gards and C Company joined the 11th Hussars.

26. Lieutenant Robertson is commemorated on the Chatby Memorial.

Chapter 3: 1916

1. *The Graphic*, 26 February 1916, p. 30.
2. *Fleetwood Chronicle* 18 February 1916, p. 2.
3. The Silver Swastika Thanks Badge had been inaugurated in 1908 and was awarded to officers who had given long and good service to the movement. Of course, the symbol had not acquired the controversy that it later acquired through its use by the Nazis.
4. *Newcastle Daily Chronicle*, 4 July 1916, p. 3.
5. *Newcastle Journal*, 23 August 1916, p. 3.
6. *Yorkshire Evening Post*, 16 November 1916, p. 5.
7. Lieutenant Hall is buried at Cite Bonjean Military Cemetery. His headstone has a moving inscription which seems to have been influenced by the poem 'In Flanders Fields'. It reads: AND FROM THE GROUND THERE BLOSSOMS RED LIFE THAT SHALL ENDLESS BE.
8. The others were the previously mentioned Roland James Walker and a William King. It has proven difficult to track down King, but Walker lost his life in 1914.
9. 2nd Lieutenant Crookes is buried at Zouave Valley Cemetery.
10. Later that year a parade of 100 scouts were inspected in Berwick by Sir Robert Baden-Powell.
11. Rifleman Prime is buried at Bulls Road Cemetery.

12. Sapper Topham is commemorated on the Thiepval Memorial.

13. Private Campbell was killed on 27 September 1915 and is commemorated on the Loos Memorial.

14. Private Darling, of Stonerigg Filters, Armadale, is commemorated on the Thiepval Memorial.

15. Lance Corporal Muirhead is buried at Bancourt British Cemetery.

16. Deck Boy Burrows is commemorated on the Plymouth Memorial.

Chapter 4: 1917

1. *Newcastle Daily Journal*, 21 April 1917, p. 9. It is somewhat insulting that the Home Office should term their request in this manner considering that Newcastle had the proud record of donating more per capita than any other comparable city to the war effort, that it was a centre of armaments and ship production, and that a huge number of men had volunteered for service from the city.

2. *Hull Daily Mail*, 3 November 1917, p. 1.

3. *Dundee Evening Telegraph*, 2 November 1917, p. 1.

4. *The Times History and Encyclopedia of the War* (Vol. XVII, 1918), p. 145.

5. Ibid.

6. Lance Corporal Finney is buried at Cambrin Churchyard Extension.

7. Private Scott is buried at Ste Catherine British Cemetery.

8. The bodies of Captain Pickering and Lieutenant Craig were subsequently moved to their current location at the Baghdad (North Gate) War Cemetery. It is possible that Lieutenant Craig was also a qualified pilot as some sources claim he had passed his test just a week before his death.

9. Midshipman (later Lieutenant) Gyles' DSC and other medals were sold at auction at Bonhams in March 2014.

10. *Cooee Magazine*, August 1918.

11. Reginald Leonard Haine recounted some of his experiences in the Peter Jackson film *They Shall Not Grow Old*.

12. Like Private Dixon, Private Mather is also commemorated on the Arras Memorial.

13. Rifleman Taylor appears to have survived the war.

14. 2nd Lieutenant Lane is commemorated on the Arras Memorial.

15. 2nd Lieutenant Lee is buried at Hooge Crater Cemetery.

16. 2nd Lieutenant Russell is commemorated at Tyne Cot.

17. 2nd Lieutenant Hamilton is commemorated at Tyne Cot.

18. 2nd Lieutenant Rose is buried at Brown's Copse Cemetery, Roeux. The village was not taken until 14 May following heavy fighting. The village and chemical works swapped hands several times until it was finally retaken by the 51st (Highland) Division on 26 August 1918.

19. 2nd Lieutenant Winser has no known grave and is commemorated on the Arras Flying Services Memorial.

20. Sergeant Bowers was an experienced aviator who had served in France from August 1916.

21. Air Mechanic 2nd Class Webb is buried at Sailly-Labourse Communal Cemetery Extension.

22. Captain Fison's sister had married a son of Lieutenant-Colonel Elliot.

23. Private Bailey is commemorated on the Arras Memorial.

24. Apprentice Temlett is commemorated on the Tower Hill Memorial.

25. This was the second wartime loss for the parents of Private Curzon. His younger brother, Rifleman Frederick Barton Curzon (33) of 18 King's Royal Rifle Corps had died at Spencer Street Military Hospital, Keighley, on 12th February 1917.

26. *Wigan Observer and District Advertiser*, 1 September 1917, p. 8.

27. Like so many who were buried on the battlefield, Private Moore's grave was subsequently lost and he is commemorated on the Tyne Cot Memorial.

28. Private Liptrop is commemorated on the Ypres (Menin Gate) Memorial.

29. Lance Corporal Dickinson is buried at Tincourt New British Cemetery.

30. Sergeant Russell is commemorated at Tyne Cot.

31. Lieutenant McCracken was named after the prominent Irish republican, industrialist and founder of the Society of the United Irishmen. He is buried at Kantara War Memorial Cemetery.

32. Private Tugwell is buried at Ecoust Military Cemetery.
33. 2nd Lieutenant Barnett is commemorated on the Tyne Cot Memorial.

Chapter 5: 1918

1. The wartime situation resulted in the awards of a number of these medals. In 1917, for example, twenty-four Bronze Crosses were won.
2. *The Times History and Encyclopaedia of the War* (Vol. XVIII, 1918), pp. 158-9.
3. *Surrey Advertiser*, 19 June 1918, p. 1.
4. *Staffordshire Sentinel*, 11 September 1918, p. 2.
5. *The Times History and Encyclopaedia of the War* (Vol XVII, 1918), p. 163.
6. Toye went on to have a successful career in the Army and during the Second World War was a Brigadier with the 6th Airborne Division and with General Headquarters. He retired with the rank of Brigadier and died in Tiverton in 1955.
7. Lance Corporal Paris is commemorated on the Pozieres Memorial.
8. Private Eley is commemorated on the Ploegsteert Memorial.
9. Sapper Mills is buried at Bertenacre Military Cemetery.
10. Cruickshank was one of five children. His youngest brother, John, died tragically aged 10 in 1913 when he fell from a tram while out shopping for a scout's cape. Private Percy Cruickshank is buried at Pont-du-Hem Military Cemetery.
11. Robert re-joined Lever Brothers after the war and stayed with the company for the next thirty-four years. He married and lived in Southend where he became very involved with the British Legion. In the mid-1930s he and his wife relocated to Glen Parva, Leicester. Robert served as a major in the Home Guard during the Second World War and following the war he served as chairman of the Glen Parva Parish Council. Throughout his life Robert remained in touch with his regimental association and his old comrades. Robert died in 1961.
12. Sergeant Chambers is buried at the Windmill British Cemetery.

13. 2nd Lieutenant Barclay appears to have survived the war.

14. Lance Corporal Weatherly is commemorated on the Vis-En-Artois Memorial. This memorial bears the names of 9,836 men who lost their lives from 8 August 1918 to the armistice.

15. Corporal Spurin, MM, is buried at St Sever Cemetery Extension.

Index